FAITH FACTS
Answers to Catholic Questions

Volume I

EMMAUS
ROAD
PUBLISHING

Leon J. Suprenant, Jr. and Philip C.L. Gray

*This book is dedicated to St. Nonna and
St. Francis de Sales, patrons of Information Services.*

St. Nonna lived during the difficult times of the fourth century. She was married to Gregory Nazianzen, a pagan, and bore him three children. Because of her prayers, fasting, and example, her husband was converted and became a champion of the Catholic faith. Nonna, Gregory, and their three children are all saints. One son, St. Gregory Nazianzen the Younger, is also a Father and doctor of the Church. St. Nonna's feast is August 5.

St. Francis de Sales lived in France during the Counter-Reformation. He was a bishop, confessor for kings and paupers, and prolific writer on the call of the laity to holiness. Many saints were influenced by his writings and example of faith. We celebrate the feast of St. Francis de Sales on January 24.

FAITH FACTS

Answers to Catholic Questions

Volume I

EMMAUS
ROAD
PUBLISHING

Leon J. Suprenant, Jr. and Philip C.L. Gray

Nihil Obstat
Rev. James Dunfee
Censor Librorum

Imprimatur ✠
Most Rev. Gilbert I. Sheldon, D.D., D.Min.

Copyright © 1999
Emmaus Road Publishing

Library of Congress 99-64655

Published by
Emmaus Road Publishing
a division of Catholics United for the Faith, Inc.
827 North Fourth Street
Steubenville, Ohio 43952
(800) 398-5470

On the Cover
Statues in St. Peter's Square
Copyright © 1999 Photodisc, Inc.

Cover design and layout
M. Elizabeth Hart

Copy editor
Ann Recznik

Published in the United States of America
ISBN 0-9663223-4-7

Contents

Mary

I charge you in the presence of God and of Christ Jesus who is to judge the living and the dead, and by his appearing and his kingdom: preach the word, be urgent in season and out of season, convince, rebuke, and exhort, be unfailing in patience and in teaching. For the time is coming when people will not endure sound teaching, but having itching ears they will accumulate for themselves teachers to suit their own likings, and will turn away from listening to the truth and wander into myths. As for you, always be steady, endure suffering, do the work of an evangelist, fulfil your ministry (2 Tim. 4:1-5).

H. Lyman Stebbins founded Catholics United for the Faith (CUF) in 1968 "to support, defend, and advance the efforts of the teaching Church." A convert to the Catholic faith, Mr. Stebbins left the Episcopal church to embrace what he found to be the one, true faith. The many problems and controversies that embroiled the Catholic Church in his day were heightened by the promulgation of *Humanae Vitae* in 1968. During this critical time, he found that Catholics did not know and understand their faith. This vacuum of faith fueled the controversies and allowed abuses and dissent to flourish in the Church. Mr. Stebbins founded CUF as a faithful response to Vatican II's call for an active lay apostolate. His purpose was to inform Catholics, unite Catholics, and defend the Catholic faith. In recognition of his efforts, John Cardinal O'Connor nominated Mr. Stebbins for knighthood. Pope John Paul II granted the request, and H. Lyman Stebbins became a Knight of St. Gregory the Great on January 10, 1988.

An important work of CUF has always been to inform Catholics. If properly informed, a good Catholic can defend the faith. He will also be formed in the faith as he grows in knowledge of the truth. CUF has always been responsive to requests from its members for reliable information on Catholic teaching, discipline, and piety. In an effort to improve services and reach a larger number of people, CUF President Curtis Martin established the Information Services department in 1995 with a toll-free phone line and a staff dedicated to answering questions about the Catholic faith. He also implemented the FAITH FACT program in 1996.

FAITH FACTS represent the most important way we inform members. They provide concise and easy-to-read answers to specific questions about the Catholic faith. They explain what the Church teaches on important issues of faith, morals, and discipline. FAITH FACTS also explain the reasons behind these teachings—reasons that are rooted in Scripture and Tradition. FAITH FACTS point to the source of truth and cite Sacred Scripture and the documents of the Magisterium to present the position of the Catholic Church. We also provide additional references for those who want to study the issue further. In short, our FAITH FACTS are intended to inform the mind, turn the heart to Christ, and help the individual learn where to go for further research and information on a topic.

The primary purpose of Information Services is to provide answers to the questions of CUF members. If a member contacts us with a question not answered in a FAITH FACT, or if he has a more specific question after having read a FAITH FACT, we will research his question and provide him an answer. This research is kept for further use if another person calls with the same question or a similar one. We do not limit the questions members ask to any particular subject other than the Catholic faith itself. As a result, we spend much time researching a broad range of questions and formulating answers that are easy to understand. In an effort to foster deeper faith and a greater awareness of Church teaching, we do provide limited services to non-members.

Although FAITH FACTS are usually no more than four standard pages in length, they represent hours of research. When Information Services was formally established, the accumulated research of over 25 years by CUF staff amounted to thousands of files. These are but one source of information for us. When we research questions, that information is added to our database and saved for future use. This becomes another source of information. Most importantly, the documents of the Church are our primary source. We continually turn to the Bible, the documents of the various ecumenical councils, encyclicals and other writings of the popes, the *Catechism of the Catholic Church*, and the writings of Church Fathers. We rely on Mother Church to provide the answer. It is our task simply to present it clearly and faithfully.

FAITH FACTS contain four sections. First, there is a specific question on a general topic. Then we provide a brief response. Third, we offer a discussion of the answer to the question. Finally, we provide a listing of recommended reading for further research on the topic. Within this book, the format of the FAITH FACTS is a little different. Within seven broad categories we present three or four FAITH FACTS. Each FAITH FACT is introduced by a question. Following this, the brief response and the discussion have been combined. At the end, we offer several study questions to assist readers in further consideration of the topic. At the end of the book, we offer recommended reading according to topic. The most important recommended readings are the Bible and the Catechism. Regular study of these two books will assist anyone in developing a deeper union with Christ and understanding of the one, true faith.

The effects of our FAITH FACT program reflect the intentions of our founder. By use of our FAITH FACTS, thousands of people have either converted to the Catholic faith, returned to full communion with the Church, or grown in their knowledge of the faith they already hold. Our FAITH FACTS are used for personal growth, to supplement catechetical or group study material, and to evangelize non-Catholics. Some members give them to door-to-door evangelists when they visit. We regularly receive testimonial letters from those who contact us. Some of these letters are published in our award-winning magazine, *Lay Witness*. All of them are posted in our Information Services office as a reminder that we are here to serve Christ by witnessing to the truth in charity.

Because FAITH FACTS are the backbone of Information Services, this book represents a glimpse of what CUF is all about. It is a small testimony to our founder, H. Lyman Stebbins, to the thousands of CUF members, and to the many CUF chapters that have united their prayers and efforts to better our Church in this age for the age to come. Without the zealous participation of so many men and women, CUF would not exist today.

As director of Information Services, I personally thank Mr. Stebbins and his wife, Madeleine, for their commitment to the Church and their courage to act in a time of need. I thank our president emeritus James Likoudis and all those who helped form CUF over the past 30 years. I thank our current president, Curtis Martin, who is personally responsible for establishing the Information Services department and the FAITH FACT program. I thank our board of directors, who have always been our strongest fan club. And I thank Leon Suprenant, executive director of CUF and editor of *Lay Witness*. He has given Information Services continuous encouragement and support, and has contributed substantially to the FAITH FACT program. Through his efforts, we are able to publish this book for the good of the Church.

We do not name the authors of the individual FAITH FACTS published here. This is intentional. Though some FAITH FACTS are written by an individual to answer a specific question, most are the result of accumulated research by many individuals. This dynamic collaboration within the department allows us to develop and write many FAITH FACTS on a broad range of topics. I personally thank my staff for their commitment to this research and the excellent service they provide those who contact us. I thank Tom Nash, who has been here longer than any other Information Services staff member, and who helped me "learn the ropes." I thank Suzanne Bronzi and Eric Stoutz, who provide much time and talent in researching questions and assisting our members. These three full-time staff members are the backbone of Information Services.

I also thank all the part-time interns from Franciscan University of Steubenville who have worked in Information Services. Many have come and gone. Others are still with us. All have contributed to the development of the department. Particularly, I thank Cat Clark, Dave Utsler, Rob Corzine, Steve Kellmeyer, Maria Colonna, Ian Burgess, Maria Garabis, Sara Trudeau, and David Osborne. Their assistance in answering the phones, providing research, and performing many other tasks has kept the office moving. Without their commitment to excellence, this book would not be possible.

There are many others worthy of thanks, without whose help the FAITH FACT program would not have its current breadth. Though not employed in Information Services, these men and women have contributed to the FAITH FACT program. Though only some of their work is contained in this book, the work by all is appreciated and essential to our apostolate. For their contributions, I thank Jeff Ziegler, Pat Madrid, John Kippley, Helen Valois, Patrick Lee, Ted Sri, Brian O'Neel, Mark Shea, Fr. Christopher Phillips, and the many other individuals who have provided us with information, constructive criticism, and enthusiastic encouragement.

As the apostolate of Information Services is the apostolate of CUF, I thank all the staff of CUF for their commitment to the FAITH FACT program. The *Lay Witness*, Emmaus Road Publishing, Fellowship Of Catholic University Students (FOCUS), and business office staffs are all committed in their desire to serve Christ and His Church. Their work assists us in ours. Thank you for all you do.

This book is written for the Universal Church. As the fruit of collaboration between so many people, this book represents an example of the communion of saints. We draw from the riches of our faith, the truth given by Christ through His Church. We present this treasure to men and women of our age with but one hope, to bring glory to God. At the threshold of the new millennium, it is my fervent prayer that this book will contribute to the new springtime of faith prophesied by our Holy Father, and that it will contribute to the salvation of souls for the glory of Christ and His Church.

UT IN OMNIBUS GLORIFICETUR DEUS!

—Philip C.L. Gray
Director, Information Services
Catholics United for the Faith

The Old Testament
Gen./Genesis
Ex./Exodus
Lev./Leviticus
Num./Numbers
Deut./Deuteronomy
Josh./Joshua
Judg./Judges
Ruth/Ruth
1 Sam./1 Samuel
2 Sam./2 Samuel
1 Kings/1 Kings
2 Kings/2 Kings
1 Chron./1 Chronicles
2 Chron./2 Chronicles
Ezra/Ezra
Neh./Nehemiah
Tob./Tobit
Jud./Judith
Esther/Esther
Job/Job
Ps./Psalms
Prov./Proverbs
Eccles./Ecclesiastes
Song/Song of Solomon
Wis./Wisdom
Sir./Sirach (Ecclesiasticus)
Is./Isaiah
Jer./Jeremiah

Lam./Lamentations
Bar./Baruch
Ezek./Ezekiel
Dan./Daniel
Hos./Hosea
Joel/Joel
Amos/Amos
Obad./Obadiah
Jon./Jonah
Mic./Micah
Nahum/Nahum
Hab./Habakkuk
Zeph./Zephaniah
Hag./Haggai
Zech./Zechariah
Mal./Malachi
1 Mac./1 Maccabees
2 Mac./2 Maccabees

The New Testament
Mt./Matthew
Mk./Mark
Lk./Luke
Jn./John
Acts/Acts of the Apostles
Rom./Romans
1 Cor./1 Corinthians
2 Cor./2 Corinthians
Gal./Galatians

Eph./Ephesians
Phil./Philippians
Col./Colossians
1 Thess./1 Thessalonians
2 Thess./2 Thessalonians
1 Tim./1 Timothy
2 Tim./2 Timothy
Tit./Titus
Philem./Philemon
Heb./Hebrews
Jas./James
1 Pet./1 Peter
2 Pet./2 Peter
1 Jn./1 John
2 Jn./2 John
3 Jn./3 John
Jude/Jude
Rev./Revelation (Apocalypse)

Documents of Vatican II

SC   Constitution on the Sacred Liturgy
     (*Sacrosanctum Concilium*), December 4, 1963
IM   Decree on the Means of Social Communication
     (*Inter Mirifica*), December 4, 1963
LG   Dogmatic Constitution on the Church
     (*Lumen Gentium*), November 21, 1964
OE   Decree on the Catholic Eastern Churches
     (*Orientalium Ecclesiarum*), November 21, 1964
UR   Decree on Ecumenism
     (*Unitatis Redintegratio*), November 21, 1964
CD   Decree on the Pastoral Office of Bishops in the Church
     (*Christus Dominus*), October 28, 1965
PC   Decree on the Up-to-Date Renewal of Religious Life
     (*Perfectae Caritatis*), October 28, 1965

OT   Decree on the Training of Priests
        (*Optatam Totius*), October 28, 1965

GE   Declaration on Christian Education
        (*Gravissimum Educationis*), October 28, 1965

NA   Declaration on the Relation of the Church to Non-
        Christian Religions (*Nostra Aetate*), October 28, 1965

DV   Dogmatic Constitution on Divine Revelation
        (*Dei Verbum*), November 18, 1965

AA   Decree on the Apostolate of Lay People
        (*Apostolicam Actuositatem*), November 18, 1965

DH   Declaration on Religious Liberty
        (*Dignitatis Humanae*), December 7, 1965

AG   Decree on the Church's Missionary Activity
        (*Ad Gentes Divinitus*), December 7, 1965

PO   Decree on the Ministry and Life of Priests
        (*Presbyterorum Ordinis*), December 7, 1965

GS   Pastoral Constitution on the Church in the Modern
        World (*Gaudium et Spes*), December 7, 1965

*All quotations from the documents of the Second Vatican Council are taken from Austin Flannery, O.P., ed., *Vatican II: The Conciliar and Post Conciliar Documents*, Northport, NY: Costello Publishing Co., copyright © 1975.

Other Magisterial Documents

PD   Pope Leo XIII, Encyclical Letter
        On the Study of Sacred Scripture (*Providentissimus Deus*), 1893

SP   Pope Benedict XV, Encyclical Letter
        On the Fifteenth Centenary of the Death of St. Jerome
        (*Spiritus Paraclitus*), 1920

DAS   Pope Pius XII, Encyclical Letter
        Promotion of Biblical Studies (*Divino Afflante Spiritu*), 1943

MF   Pope Paul VI, Encyclical Letter
        The Mystery of Faith (*Mysterium Fidei*), 1965

HV   Pope Paul VI, Encyclical Letter
        On Human Life (*Humanae Vitae*), 1968
GIRM   General Instruction of the Roman Missal, 1970
CT   Pope John Paul II, Apostolic Exhortation
        On Catechesis in Our Time (*Catechesi Tradendae*), 1979
FC   Pope John Paul II, Apostolic Exhortation
        The Role of the Christian Family in the Modern World
        (*Familiaris Consortio*), 1981
RMT   Pope John Paul II, Encyclical Letter
        Mother of the Redeemer (*Redemptoris Mater*), 1987
RMS   Pope John Paul II, Encyclical Letter
        Mission of the Redeemer (*Redemptoris Missio*), 1990
VS   Pope John Paul II, Encyclical Letter
        The Splendor of Truth (*Veritatis Splendor*), 1993
EV   Pope John Paul II, Encyclical Letter
        The Gospel of Life (*Evangelium Vitae*), 1995
FR   Pope John Paul II, Encyclical Letter
        Faith and Reason (*Fides et Ratio*), 1998

Catechism of the Catholic Church

Throughout the text, the *Catechism of the Catholic Church* (United States Catholic Conference—Libreria Editrice Vaticana, 1994, as revised in the 1997 Latin typical edition) will be cited simply as "Catechism."

Code of Canon Law

All quotations from the current (1983) Code of Canon Law are taken from *Code of Canon Law, Latin-English Edition*, Washington: Canon Law Society of America, copyright © 1983. Throughout the text, passages from the 1983 Code will be cited simply by reference to "canon."

Chapter 1

THIS IS MY BODY
Christ's Real Presence in the Eucharist

Does the Catholic Church teach that we actually eat the body of Christ and drink His blood when we receive Holy Communion?

Yes. The Catholic Church has always taught that in the Most Blessed Sacrament of the Eucharist, the body and blood, together with the soul and divinity, of our Lord Jesus—the whole Christ—is truly, really, and substantially present. This teaching is rooted in Scripture, taught by the Fathers and doctors of the Church, and reaffirmed by popes and ecumenical councils throughout Church history. This teaching is summarized in the *Catechism of the Catholic Church* (nos. 1373-81).

Bread from Heaven

As the Old Testament attests, almighty God prepared His chosen people for the coming of Christ. He established His covenant with Abraham, confirmed the covenant with Isaac, and raised up a people through the sons of Jacob. When the Israelites were made slaves in Egypt, He led them out of slavery. This rescue from Egypt was just the beginning. Only after many years of trials and hardships would the people finally reach their destination. To prevent them from starving in the desert, God gave the people manna—"bread from heaven" (cf. Ex. 16:4 *et seq.*). He also led them by means of a cloud that hovered over the ark of the covenant (cf. Num. 9:15-23). These were two very tangible ways that the Lord demonstrated He was truly with His people.

As much as God cared for the Israelites in the desert, even more does He provide for His pilgrim Church today, by giving us His Son as our daily bread. As Jesus Himself said,

I am the bread of life. Your fathers ate the manna in the wilderness, and they died.

This is the bread which comes down from heaven, that a man may eat of it and not die. I am the living bread which came down from heaven; if any one eats of this bread, he will live for ever; and the bread which I shall give for the life of the world is my flesh (Jn. 6:48-51).

There are those today who accept the authority of the Bible but question whether Jesus was speaking literally in the Eucharistic passages, especially John 6. The Greek text itself evidences the Church's constant understanding. In John 6:49, Jesus begins His teaching by first referring to eating manna. He uses the word 'ἔφαγον,[1] which means "eat" or "consume." This verb can be used literally or figuratively. He then refers to Himself as the new manna, the living bread from heaven, of which those who eat will live forever. In this context, He uses the same word because of the figurative connection with manna.

After verse 52, when the Jews dispute His teaching, Jesus uses more emphatic language to clarify His teaching and address their concerns. He employs two techniques. First, He abandons any figurative association with manna. He no longer speaks of simply "eating," but of "eating flesh and drinking blood." He ends His explanation by stating, "This is the bread which came down from heaven, *not such as your fathers ate and died*" (Jn. 6:58). Second, later in the discourse Jesus began using the word τρώγων,[2] which is rendered "gnaw" or "chew." The verb τρώγω is rarely used figuratively, and in the context used by Christ is evidently to be taken literally.

Many of the disciples had left everything to follow Jesus. They had just witnessed a miraculous multiplication of loaves (Jn. 6:1-14) and probably heard about His walking on water (Jn. 6:16-21), yet now they walk away from Jesus on account of this teaching (Jn. 6:66). This reaction simply would not make sense if Jesus were speaking only figuratively or symbolically.

---

[1] Aorist of ἐσθίω (esthiō).
[2] Present participle of τρώγω (trōgō).

Witness of the Church
Even more telling is the fact that during Christianity's first thousand years there was virtually unanimous acceptance of the Church's teaching on the Real Presence by faithful Christians. No one taught that the presence of Christ was only symbolic until Ratramnus (d. 868) and, more notably, Berengarius of Tours (d. 1088). The Church firmly rejected the teachings of both.

Conversely, there are many early Fathers of the Church who affirm Christ's Real Presence in the Eucharist. For example, we have the writing of Saint Ignatius of Antioch (d. 110), whose witness is of unique importance since he was a disciple of Saint John, the author of the fourth Gospel. If there were any confusion as to the proper interpretation of John 6, surely Saint Ignatius could clarify the matter. Yet he never wrote that Jesus was speaking figuratively. Rather, he wrote, "I desire the Bread of God, which is the Flesh of Jesus Christ."[3] Elsewhere he wrote that

[t]hose who hold heterodox opinions on the grace of Jesus Christ which has come to us . . . do not confess that the Eucharist is the Flesh of our Savior Jesus Christ, Flesh which suffered for our sins and which the Father, in His goodness, raised up again.[4]

Then there is the witness of Saint Justin Martyr (d. 165) from his *First Apology*:

For not as common bread nor common drink do we receive these; but since Jesus Christ our Savior was made incarnate by the word of God and had both flesh and blood for our salvation, so too, as we have been taught, the food which has been made into the Eucharist by the Eucharistic prayer set down by Him, and by the change of which our blood and flesh is nourished, is both the flesh and the blood of that incarnated Jesus.[5]

---

[3] Letter to the Romans, 7, 3, as translated in William A. Jurgens, ed., *The Faith of the Early Fathers*, vol. 1 (Collegeville, MN: The Liturgical Press, 1970), 22.
[4] Letter to the Smyrnaeans, 7, *ibid.*, 25.
[5] *First Apology*, 66, *ibid.*, 55.

Saint Cyril of Jerusalem (d. 386), at the end of a sermon on the Christian faith, taught:

[T]hat which seems to be bread, is not bread, though it tastes like it, but the Body of Christ, and that which seems to be wine, is not wine, though it too tastes as such, but the Blood of Christ. . . . [D]raw inner strength by receiving this bread as spiritual food and your soul will rejoice.[6]

Christ's presence is clearly the work of God. In the words of Saint John Chrysostom (d. 407):

The priest standing there in the place of Christ says these words but their power and grace are from God. "This is My Body," he says, and these words transform what lies before him.[7]

This teaching has been repeated over and over again by the great Fathers, doctors, and saints of the Church through the centuries.

In the sixteenth century, when the Church's constant teaching was called into question by the Protestant reformers, the Council of Trent solemnly reaffirmed Our Lord's Real Presence in the Eucharist:

But since Christ, our Redeemer, has said that that is truly His own body which He offered under the species of bread [cf. Mt. 26:26 ff.; Mk. 14:22 ff.; Lk. 22:19 ff.; 1 Cor. 11:24 ff.], it has always been a matter of conviction in the Church of God, and now this holy Synod declares it again, that by the consecration of the bread and wine a conversion takes place of the whole sub-stance of bread into the substance of the body of Christ our Lord, and of the whole substance of the wine into the substance of His blood. This conversion is appropriately and properly called transubstantiation by the Catholic Church [can. 2].[8]

---

[6] As quoted in MF 48.
[7] As quoted in ibid., 49.
[8] Council of Trent, session XIII, "Decree on the Most Holy Eucharist," chapter 4, as quoted in Henry Denzinger, ed., The Sources of Catholic Dogma (Powers Lake, ND: Marian House, 1957), trans. by Roy J. Deferrari, 267-68. Cf. Catechism, no. 1376.

When the words of consecration are spoken by the priest (cf. Mt. 26:26-29; Mk. 14:22-25; Lk. 22:17-19; 1 Cor. 11:23-25), Christ is true to His word: Through the action of the Holy Spirit, the bread and wine are transformed into the body and blood of Christ. Through the Eucharist, we are, among other things, nourished and strengthened in our Christian pilgrimage, and experience Christ's assurance that He will be with us always (cf. Mt. 28:20).

Gift of Faith

Pope John Paul II has said that there is today a "crisis of faith" (RM 2), and declining belief in and reverence toward the Real Presence is perhaps *the* case in point. Yet we know that the ability to accept this "hard teaching" (cf. Jn. 6:60) is possible only through the gift of faith. As Saint Bonaventure teaches:

> There is no difficulty about Christ's presence in the Eucharist as in a sign, but that He is truly present in the Eucharist as He is in heaven, this is most difficult. Therefore to believe this is especially meritorious.[9]

When discussing our faith with Christians who aren't Catholic, we must build upon our shared love for Christ. Their willingness to follow Christ as Lord is the essential pathway to accepting Christ's teaching about the Eucharist (cf. Jn. 6:67-69). If Jesus is truly present in the Eucharist, then He is truly there for all. A shared faith in Christ will lead us to a shared love of Him in the Blessed Sacrament.

Let us pray to our Eucharistic Lord, then, for an increase of faith for ourselves and for all, so that, united as brothers and sisters in the Lord, we may together share in the one heavenly banquet.

---

[9] As quoted in MF 20.

Questions for Reflection
or Group Discussion

1. What is my attitude toward the Blessed Sacrament? How do my thoughts, words, and actions bear witness to the Real Presence?

2. How does the constant teaching of the Church affirm the biblical evidence for Christ's presence in the Eucharist?

3. What can I do, with God's grace, to foster greater Eucharistic faith and devotion in myself, my family, and my friends and colleagues?

Chapter 2

NO BULL
Papal Authority and Our Response

What is the origin and purpose of papal authority? What obedience is due the Pope by the People of God?

Papal authority has divine origin. The Lord made Simon alone, whom He named Peter, the "rock" of His Church. He gave him the keys of His Church and instituted him shepherd of the whole flock.

The Pope, Bishop of Rome and Peter's successor, "is the perpetual and visible source and foundation of the unity both of the bishops and of the whole company of the faithful" (LG 23). "For the Roman Pontiff, by reason of his office as Vicar of Christ . . . and as pastor of the entire Church, has full, supreme and universal power over the whole Church, a power which he can always exercise unhindered" (LG 22).

When the Pope speaks on matters concerning faith and morals, or even Church discipline, the faithful are bound by divine obligation to obey. As faithful Catholics, we must embrace his pronouncements with docility. Only in this way will our hearts be open to the truth found within.

Christ established the Church in such manner that her authority is part of her nature. He established her as "the pillar and foundation of truth" (1 Tim. 3:15) and gave her divine authority to preserve unity and truth (cf. Mt. 28:18-20).

Divine Origin of the Papacy

As Isaiah 43:1 points out, the act of naming claims the one named. This "claiming" includes the recognition of a particular purpose or mission. Scripture makes this evident in the passages about God's naming of Abraham and Israel (Gen. 17:5, 32:29). When Nebuchadnezzar appointed Mattaniah as king of Judah, he changed Mattaniah's name to Zedekiah as a sign that the new king's authority came from the king of Babylon (2 Kings 24:17). In this same way, Jesus claims Peter and his successors to be the visible source of authority in His Church.

Our Lord said to Simon:

> And I tell you, you are Peter, and on this rock I will build my church, and the powers of death shall not prevail against it. I will give you the keys of the kingdom of heaven, and whatever you bind on earth shall be bound in heaven, and whatever you loose on earth shall be loosed in heaven (Mt. 16:18-19).

Until Jesus named Peter, Scripture only referred to God as "rock," in the sense of an unfailing bulwark against the powers of evil. By making Peter the "rock" of His Church, Christ grants him divine authority over the Church on earth as His universal Vicar. He gives Peter divine power to fulfill his mission. The name "Rock" identifies Peter's mission with the authority of Christ. The primary function of this authority is unity (cf. Lk. 22:31-32).

Because of Baptism, the Catholic faithful have a divine obligation to maintain unity with the Catholic Church. Profession of faith, ecclesiastical governance, and the sacraments constitute the visible bonds of unity between the Catholic faithful and the Church of Christ ruled by the Pope and bishops in union with him. As Christ conveyed to Peter and the first apostles, if any of these bonds of unity are lacking, unity with the Church is lacking: "He who hears you hears me, and he who rejects you rejects me, and he who rejects me rejects him who sent me" (Lk. 10:16).

By divine will, unity demands obedience to lawful authority in the Church. Because the Pope is the supreme authority in the Church and has the specific obligation to ensure unity of faith, obedience to him is an act of the will required of the Catholic faithful. Such obedience expresses the faith by which we are saved.

Expressions of Papal Authority

To understand papal authority, we must understand the authoritative nature of the deposit of faith. Jesus Christ is the fullness of all Revelation. He is the Second Person of the Blessed Trinity, the Word made flesh. Through Him, all have access to the Father through the Holy Spirit. Through His words and deeds, especially His death and Resurrection, He has entrusted the sum total of all truth to His bride, the Church. The fullness of Christ's Revelation is the one deposit of faith. Because it is given by Christ, the deposit of faith is inerrant, unchangeable, and has application in every culture for all ages. Being the source of all divinely revealed truth, the one deposit of faith is the wellspring from which all doctrines and definitions of the faith flow. To summarize,

> All that is contained in the written word of God or in tradition, that is, in the one deposit of faith entrusted to the Church and also proposed as divinely revealed either by the solemn magisterium of the Church or by its ordinary and universal magisterium, must be believed with divine and catholic faith; it is manifested by the common adherence of the Christian faithful under the leadership of the sacred magisterium; therefore, all are bound to avoid any doctrines whatever which are contrary to these truths (canon 750).

To ensure unity of faith, the Magisterium of the Church has the task of interpreting the deposit of faith and applying it to specific times and circumstances. The Magisterium of the Church sometimes offers a solemn definition on a matter pertaining to faith or morals. These definitions provide absolute certainty that the teaching belongs to the deposit of faith. In other instances, the Magisterium identifies the truth found in the deposit of faith without providing a solemn definition. In these instances, though not solemnly defined, the teaching cannot be changed because it is true. These teachings are infallible.

If the Pope appeals to the deposit of faith, whether by pronouncement of the solemn or ordinary Magisterium, the teaching must be believed with divine and catholic faith. Additionally, the manner in which he speaks requires a certain docile acceptance by the Catholic faithful. The level of docility depends on the type of pronouncement and the manner in which it is given.

Solemn and Ordinary Magisterium

Pronouncements that demand full assent of divine and catholic faith require precise wording. These magisterial teachings fall into two categories: *solemn* and *ordinary*.

When, in exercise of the solemn Magisterium, the Pope speaks *ex cathedra*, the faithful are bound to accept the teaching with divine and catholic faith and must avoid any doctrines that are contrary to these truths. The exercise of the solemn Magisterium by the Pope occurs when he proclaims with a definitive act that a doctrine of faith or morals is infallible teaching. This infallibility derives from the authority Christ entrusted to His Church, and extends as far as the deposit of faith itself, as well as to doctrinal elements needed to preserve, expound, or observe this deposit and the precepts of the natural law (cf. 1 Tim 6:20; Catechism, nos. 2035-36, 2051).

Infallible character is not given to a document as a whole, but only to that portion which explicitly defines a doctrine of faith or morals. The wording of such definitions must reflect the intention to define infallibly. It must be precise and clear. An excellent example of this type of wording can be found in an apostolic constitution of Pius XII, *Munificentissimus Deus*. This pronouncement defines the Assumption of Mary and states:

> [B]y the authority of our Lord Jesus Christ, of the Blessed Apostles Peter and Paul, and by our own authority, we pronounce, declare, and define it to be a divinely revealed dogma: that the Immaculate Mother of God, the ever Virgin Mary, having completed the course of her earthly life, was assumed body and soul into heavenly glory.

> Hence if anyone, which God forbid, should dare willfully to deny or to call into doubt that which we have defined, let him know that he has fallen away completely from the divine and Catholic Faith.[1]

---

[1] Pope Pius XII, Apostolic Constitution Defining the Dogma of the Assumption *Munificentissimus Deus* (1950), nos. 44-45.

More frequently, the Pope appeals to the deposit of faith by use of the ordinary Magisterium. This occurs when he definitively confirms a teaching as pertaining to the deposit of faith. Examples of such teachings include: male-only priesthood (Pope John Paul II's apostolic letter, *Ordinatio Sacerdotalis*), the intrinsic evils of abortion and euthanasia (Pope John Paul II's encyclical letter, *Evangelium Vitae*), and the intrinsic evil of contraception (Pope Paul VI's encyclical letter, *Humanae Vitae*).

While these documents do not contain explicit definitions as noted above, their wording clearly appeals to the authority of the Pope to confirm what proceeds from the deposit of faith. As such, these teachings enjoy infallibility and demand the assent of divine and catholic faith.

An excellent example of this type of pronouncement is found in *Humanae Vitae*. Pope Paul VI did not use definitive language appealing to the solemn Magisterium. He did appeal to the ordinary Magisterium and the pronouncement's basis in the deposit of faith and the natural law:

> It can be foreseen that this teaching will perhaps not be easily received by all. . . . [Y]et she does not because of this cease to proclaim with humble firmness the entire moral law, both natural and evangelical. Of such laws the Church was not the author, nor consequently can she be their arbiter; she is only their depositary and their interpreter, without ever being able to declare to be licit that which is not so by reason of its intimate and unchangeable opposition to the true good of man (HV 18).

Because these teachings have not been proposed or confirmed through a solemn definition, many mistakenly believe that such teachings can be revised. As Archbishop Tarcisio Bertone, the secretary of the Congregation for the Doctrine of the Faith, explains:

> [T]he truth and irreformability of a doctrine depend on the *depositum fidei* [deposit of the faith], transmitted by the Scripture and Tradition, while infallibility refers only to the degree of certitude of an act of magisterial teaching. . . . In the light of these considerations, it seems a pseudo-problem to

wonder whether this papal act of *confirming* a teaching of the ordinary, universal Magisterium is infallible or not. In fact, although it is not *per se a dogmatic definition* . . . a papal pronouncement of *confirmation* enjoys the same infallibility as the teaching of the ordinary, universal Magisterium, which includes the Pope not as a mere Bishop but as the Head of the Episcopal College.[2]

Authentic Magisterium

The authentic Magisterium represents the Pope's authority to teach. The Pope exercises the authentic Magisterium whenever he teaches on faith and morals. Whether the document contains infallible statements or not, the document as a whole carries this authority. "[T]he faithful 'are to adhere to it with religious assent' which, though distinct from the assent of faith, is nonetheless an extension of it" (Catechism, no. 892, quoting LG 25). This level of obedience is further defined in canon 752 of the Code of Canon Law as "a religious respect of intellect and will. . . . [T]herefore the Christian faithful are to take care to avoid whatever is not in harmony with that teaching."

The Pope commonly uses encyclicals to communicate such pronouncements. *Humanae Vitae*, for example, contains teachings of the ordinary Magisterium that require the assent of divine and catholic faith. However, the primary intent of the encyclical was not to define such teachings, for they had already been recognized by the Church. Rather, the intent was to lead the faithful in a better understanding of Revelation and apply the deposit of faith to the particular circumstances of our time. The faithful are obligated to embrace such teaching with religious assent of intellect and will and avoid whatever is not in harmony with the encyclical as a whole.

---

[2] Archbishop Tarcisio Bertone, S.D.B., "Magisterial Documents and Public Dissent," *L'Osservatore Romano* (English ed., January 25, 1997), 6-7, original emphasis. See also Pope John Paul II, Apostolic Letter To Protect the Faith *Ad Tuendam Fidem* (1998), which reiterates the faithful's obligation to assent to the teachings of both the ordinary and solemn Magisterium of the Church with a "divine and Catholic faith."

Constitutions and Decrees

Canon 754 of the Code of Canon Law identifies another level of obedience pertaining to constitutions and decrees issued to establish discipline and answer erroneous opinions. While not demanding a full assent of faith, these documents call for an assent of will that flows from faith, and the faithful are obliged to observe them. One example of this type of pronouncement would be the apostolic constitution *Divinus Perfectionis Magister*, which sets forth the norms for beatification and canonization. Another example is the apostolic constitution *Sacrae Disciplinae Leges*, which was used to promulgate the Code of Canon Law for the Latin Church. As the means of promulgating the Code, this constitution binds the faithful to observe these laws and disciplines.

Obedience to Christ demands obedience to the Pope. There is no authority on earth who can legitimately amend decrees or judgments of the Pope. Other than God Himself, there is no authority above the Pope. Obedience to him must flow, not so much from an understanding of faith, but from faith itself, which guides and nourishes the will. Thus, whether dealing with infallible doctrine or a decree that concerns a Church discipline, obedience to the Pope exemplifies a unity of faith founded on the will of Christ.

_____*SideBar*___

The Papal Office

Pope John Paul II is the 264th pope in the history of Christendom. One of the earliest witnesses to the unbroken chain of papal succession is Saint Irenaeus (c. 140-c. 202), the second Bishop of Lyons, who wrote:

The blessed Apostles, having founded and built up the Church, they handed over the office of the episcopate [of Rome] to Linus. Paul makes mention of this Linus in the Epistle to Timothy. To him succeeded Anencletus . . . Clement . . . Evaristus . . . Alexander . . . Sixtus . . . Telesphorus . . . Hyginus . . . Pius . . . Anicetus . . . Soter . . . and now, in the

twelfth place after the apostles, the lot of the episcopate has
fallen to Eleutherus. In this order, and by the teaching of the
Apostles handed down in the Church, the preaching of the
truth has come to us.

—*Against the Heresies*, 3,3,3

Questions for Reflection
or Group Discussion

1. Do I believe in everything the Church teaches, or just those
teachings I agree with or find easy to accept?

2. Everyone is tempted to doubt. Do I give in to this temptation?
What can I do to strengthen my faith, especially during times
of temptation?

3. The word "docile" literally means "teachable." Do I have the
virtue of docility? Do I accept the God-given authority of the
Church and allow her to teach me?

Chapter 3

ALL IN THE FAMILY
The Communion of Saints

What is the communion of saints?

The communion of saints is the intimate union that exists among all the disciples of Christ. This communion is known as the Mystical Body of Christ: the Family of God consisting of the faithful on earth (the Church Militant or pilgrim Church), the holy souls in purgatory undergoing spiritual cleansing (the Church Suffering), and the saints in heaven (the Church Triumphant). This union of believers joins us in Christ, our source of grace and life, and calls us to love and pray for one another as members of His body. Therefore, we can ask for the prayers of the saints in heaven, and we can also can also pray for people on earth and those in purgatory (Catechism, nos. 946-62).

The doctrine of the communion of saints was taught by the apostles, both in the Scriptures and the Tradition they handed down in words and practice. It is explicitly contained in the Apostles' Creed. The Church reaffirmed this teaching at the Second Council of Nicea (787) and further addressed it at the Councils of Florence (1438-45), Trent (1545-63), and Vatican II (1962-65).

This *communion* refers to the bond of unity among the followers of Christ. Such a bond is possible because, as believers in Christ, we become children of God (1 Jn. 3:1), members of His family (Rom. 8:14-17), with divine life bestowed on us through Baptism (Jn. 3:3-5). The apostles teach us that through Baptism we become "fellow heirs with Christ" (Rom. 8:17) and "partakers of the divine nature" (2 Pet. 1:4). Saint Paul states that this union of the faithful, brought about by the Holy Spirit in Baptism, is so complete that we are actually members of a single body, *Christ's own body* (cf. 1 Cor. 12:12-27).

The communion of saints is based on four essential points:

- All Christians are members of Christ's body and one another (Rom. 12:5; 1 Cor. 12:27).
- Jesus has only one body (Eph. 4:4; Col. 3:15).
- Death cannot separate Christians from Christ or from one another (Rom. 8:35-39; cf. Lk. 20:37-38).
- Christians are bound in mutual love (Jn. 13:34-35; Rom. 12:10).

Family Ties

In John 15:1-5, Jesus tells us that He is the vine and we are the branches. As branches are connected to a vine, participating in a single life, we are connected to Jesus and to one another in His Mystical Body. Saint Paul speaks many times about the importance of this unity in one body (e.g., 1 Cor. 12:12-27; Rom. 12:4-16). As members of the same family, we are able to pray for one another and to ask others—including the saints in heaven—to pray for us. Nothing, not even death, can break that union between Christ and His body and the members with one another (cf. Rom. 8:35-39). Everyone who is "in Christ" (2 Cor. 5:17) participates in His life not only on earth, but even more fully in the glory of heaven.

In a human family, members love one another, are concerned for one another's well-being and growth, turn to one another in times of joy and sorrow, and intercede for one another in times of trial and distress. Therefore, it is fitting that in God's supernatural family, Christians are called to love one another and be concerned for the good of one another, turning to one another for inspiration and intercession in times of need. Saint Paul himself asks for the intercession of others (e.g., Rom. 15:30; Col. 4:3). He further stresses the mutual need of all Christians for one another:

> The eye cannot say to the hand, "I have no need of you," nor again the head to the feet, "I have no need of you.". . . If one member [of the body] suffers, all suffer together; if one member is honored, all rejoice together" (1 Cor. 12:21, 26).

We cannot say, then, that one "does not need" the saints in heaven or the souls in purgatory, because they too are members of the Body of Christ.

The Bible speaks of the prayers of angels and other saints in heaven, including prayer offered from and for others, and also tells us of the martyrs' praying for justice to come upon the earth (e.g., Rev. 6:9-11; Tob. 12:12). The angels and saints are concerned with earthly events (e.g., Ps. 91:11-12; Lk. 15:7; Rev. 5:8). If they were not concerned, they would be guilty of a lack of charity for their brothers on earth, because charity means desiring and seeking to bring about the ultimate good of others. Such a gross violation of love is simply not possible in heaven (cf. 1 Jn. 3:10, 14-15; 4:7-11).

Alive in Christ

Some object that the Catholic position on intercessory prayer is the same as *necromancy*, that is, calling upon the spirits of the dead to find out the future or obtain other information. Necromancy is a grave sin that, far from fostering communion, shows a lack of faith and trust in God. Necromancy was punishable by death under the Mosaic law (Lev. 19:31, 20:6). Some of the early Israelites practiced necromancy, including Saul (1 Sam. 28:3, 8-14), and they were punished severely for doing so (1 Sam. 28:17-19). This practice offended God (2 Kings 21:6) and led to the destruction of Israel.

Catholics do not practice necromancy, which is explicitly forbidden by the Church (cf. Catechism, nos. 2115-17). Rather, they ask for the prayers of the saints to foster communion in the Family of God.

Seeking the intercession of the saints is not necromancy for two reasons. First, necromancers are usually trying to receive information that they do not have, such as what will happen in the future. Asking the saints to pray for us, however, is not a form of divination or fortune-telling.

Second, necromancers are also trying to bring back and control the souls of dead people. Catholics, on the contrary, believe that those who have died in God's grace are not dead but truly alive, and are able to help us by their prayers. As Jesus says, "[Moses] calls the Lord the God of Abraham and the God of Isaac and the God of Jacob. Now he is not the God of the dead, but of the living; for all live to him" (Lk. 20:37-38).

According to Jesus, death cannot separate the faithful—such as Abraham, Isaac, and Jacob—from God. And, if they are alive to God, they must be alive to us through Him as members of His one body. *Otherwise, contrary to what Saint Paul says, Christ's victory over death was incomplete, and His body is not truly one.*

Idol Chatter

Some believe that asking the saints in heaven to pray for us is a form of *idolatry*. The Catholic Church does not worship any person other than God, who created everyone and everything. The Church may offer praise and honor to Mary and the other saints, who are great disciples of the Lord, but she worships God alone.

The saints are honored and blessed by God and therefore worthy of our respect, and they serve as role models for Christians to emulate (e.g., Phil. 3:17; 4:8-9). This is not idolatry as long as they are distinguished from God. For example, Abraham the patriarch bows down before angels of the Lord and Nathan the prophet bows down before David the king of Israel—in due reverence, not idolatry (cf. Gen. 18:2; 1 Kings 1:23). We ask saints to bring our needs before Our Heavenly Father, for "[t]he prayer of a righteous man has great power in its effects" (Jas. 5:16).

Similarly, some claim that the phrase "praying to saints" indicates that Catholics are treating the saints as if they were gods, and thus committing idolatry. This reflects a common misunderstanding of the English language. "Pray" historically meant nothing more than "to ask" or "to make a humble request." Until modern times, this word was never used exclusively as a request to God. Rather, it was often used in common speech between two people, as in the sentence: "I pray you, may words have more than one meaning?" It is in the older sense that Catholics "pray to the saints," which merely means asking for their intercession on our behalf.

One Mediator

Another common objection is that asking the saints to pray for us violates the Bible's teaching in 1 Timothy 2:5, which states there is one Mediator between God and men, Jesus Christ. When read in context, however, Saint Paul clearly states that *this is the reason Christians should pray for others*, rather than a reason against it: "I urge that supplications, prayers, intercessions, and thanksgivings be made for all men. . . . This is good and it is acceptable in the sight of God our Savior. . ." (1 Tim. 2:1, 3).

Jesus' mediation between God and man is based on the Incarnation, the truth that He is both fully God and fully man. No one else can mediate in this way, which is why it is correct to say "there is one Mediator." Christians can and do, however, *participate* in Jesus' mediation in a lesser and dependent way, just as they share in His one eternal priesthood (1 Pet. 2:5), because they are members of His body and "coworkers with God" (cf. 1 Cor. 3:9).

All Christians are called to unite their prayers, supplications, and intercessions to those of Jesus. Jesus' mediation is what makes the mediation of other Christians possible, just as His priesthood makes the ordained priesthood and the priesthood of believers possible. Christians intercede on earth for one another without diminishing Christ's unique mediation. The same holds true in heaven. All prayer, whether on earth or in heaven, comes to the Father through Christ. Just as the one Creator shares His creative role with couples in procreation, or delegates His authority to Peter and the apostles, Christ shares His mediation with the saints, who are members of His own body.

Another commonly held objection is that the saints cannot hear us. Yet, Christ our Mediator enables us to communicate with members of His body. The saints in heaven are intimately connected to us through Christ, like branches on a vine. Scripture passages such as Luke 15:7 demonstrate that the angels and saints in heaven clearly do know and care about what is happening on earth. After all, the saints surround us like "a cloud of witnesses" (Heb. 12:1).

A final common objection is that no human being in this life can simultaneously hear numerous prayers, so how can a human being, even if a glorified saint, do so elsewhere? The answer is that heaven escapes the limitations of time and space that we experience in this life on earth. The Bible teaches that those in heaven can intercede for many, and bring their prayers before the throne of God (cf. Rev. 5:8; 8:3-4).

God's Love: A Consuming Fire

What about prayer for the souls in purgatory? Most objections here are based on a disbelief in purgatory. But these objections are answered by the Bible, which affirms the value of prayer for those who have died:

> [Judas] took up a collection, man by man . . . and sent it to Jerusalem to provide for a sin offering[1] [for soldiers who had died]. In doing this he acted very well and honorably, taking account of the resurrection. For if he were not expecting that those who had fallen would rise again, it would have been superfluous and foolish to pray for the dead. But if he was looking to the splendid reward that is laid up for those who fall asleep in godliness, it was a holy and pious thought (2 Mac. 12:43-45).

Some Christians do not accept 2 Maccabees as part of the Bible, although it has always been part of the canon recognized by the Church. But those who do not accept this book as scriptural must still admit that it is a history of the Jewish people that reflects their religious beliefs two centuries before Christ. Jews prayed for those who had died then and they still do today, and ancient Christian liturgies and tomb inscriptions continued the practice. Likewise, Saint Paul prays that his friend Onesiphorus, who seems to have died, will obtain

---

[1] A "sin offering," in this context, is the removal of the temporal (not eternal) consequences of sin that remain after sin is forgiven, which may be rectified in "the age to come" (Mt. 12:32; cf. 1 Cor. 3:12-15).

mercy on the last day (2 Tim. 1:16-18). It is certainly acceptable to pray for souls in purgatory, for they too are members of the Body of Christ (cf. Catechism, nos. 1030-32).

All the faithful who are alive in God's grace, on earth, in purgatory, and in heaven, are children of God, brothers and sisters of one another, and members of the single Body of Christ. Because we are one communion and one body, we need each other. It is fitting for us to ask for prayers and offer prayers for one another to build up the Body of Christ and advance the kingdom of God.

_____ *SideBar*___

Communion in Spiritual Goods

All those united to Christ are also united to one another. We participate in the treasury of riches with which Christ has endowed His Church.

Communion in the faith. What we believe is the faith of the Church, received from the apostles and their successors. Faith is a "pearl of great price" (cf. Mt. 13:45-46) that we are to share with others.

Communion of the sacraments. The merits of Christ's saving work are communicated to members of His body through the sacraments, beginning with the waters of Baptism and culminating in the Eucharist, which signifies and brings about our unity in Christ.

Communion of charisms. The Holy Spirit distributes special graces to all the faithful for the building up of the Church.

Communion of worldly goods. Christians should be ready and eager to come to the aid to those in need, recognizing that the goods of the earth are intended for the entire human family.

Communion in charity. Since we are really united with our brothers and sisters in Christ, the least of our acts done in charity strengthen our communion, just as every sin harms this communion. "If we love one another, God abides in us and his love is perfected in us" (1 Jn. 5:12).

—adapted from Catechism, nos. 949-53

Questions for Reflection
or Group Discussion

1. Do I experience the Church as a reality that is larger than my own parish family? What can I do to heighten my awareness of the needs of Christians in other parts of the world?

2. Review Catechism, nos. 1030-32. The doctrine of purgatory is difficult or even embarrassing to some Catholics who don't understand what the Church teaches. Am I able to explain this teaching to others? Do I need further explanation myself? (Chapter XIII of *Catholic for a Reason: Scripture and the Mystery of the Family of God* and CUF's FAITH FACT on purgatory are good starting points.)

3. Who are my patron saints? Do I have a special devotion to a particular saint? How do I understand the role of the saints in my own personal pilgrimage to heaven?

DEFENDING OUR RITES
Constructively Dealing with Liturgical Abuse

How do I know if liturgical abuse occurs in my parish? What can I do about it?

Many people contact us with questions about specific acts within the liturgy that could be abuses. In most instances, the issues are easily addressed by applying certain principles and norms of liturgical law. This FAITH FACT provides general information that will allow readers in most instances to determine whether a given act is an abuse and how they can properly address it.

Unfortunately, many abuses occur in the liturgy today. There are many reasons for these abuses. Some people refuse to accept the legitimate authority of the Church to establish binding norms for the liturgy. They refuse to follow the liturgical guidelines and honor the documents issued by legitimate authority. Others, because of poor formation, do not know what those guidelines are. Still others do not understand the public liturgies, the signs used in them, and the importance of consistency in worship within a particular rite of the Church.

Finally, and most tragically, many people have lost a sense of the sacred. They view the Mass as an obligation imposed by men rather than as an opportunity to worship the one, true God through the mysterious sacrifice of Jesus Christ, the Son of God. A rather large number of Catholics do not believe in the Real Presence. Because they do not believe Jesus is really present in the fullness of His divinity and humanity, they find no need to worship as the Church intends. That is, during Mass they focus on themselves, one another, or only the humanity of Jesus. They have lost a sense of the sacred.

In most cases, a combination of these reasons contributes to abuses. Those who feel offended often do not know what to do. It is important to understand certain principles that govern the liturgies of the Church. Using these principles, one should carefully discern (a) whether the act is an abuse, (b) the seriousness of the act, (c) whether it is worth addressing, and (d) what constructive steps may be taken.

Public Prayer vs. Private Devotion

The liturgies of the Church are public prayers. That means they belong by right to the Church herself and are governed by special norms particular to the specific liturgy. They require official representation for the worship to occur. In most cases, this representation must be by a man in Holy Orders, but in some cases it may be a religious or a member of the laity. The norms governing the celebration will make this clear (cf. canon 834 §2). These liturgies include the Mass, the celebration of sacraments outside of Mass (e.g., Baptisms), the Liturgy of the Hours, and also certain blessings (ashes, blessing on the memorial of Saint Blase) and other liturgical acts (Eucharistic processions, Benediction, etc.). The celebration of Mass requires a priest, but Communion services may be conducted by deacons or properly deputed laity. The Church encourages the laity to pray the Liturgy of the Hours in the privacy of their homes, but it remains a public prayer of the Church.[1] If offered in a public place, it should be led by "[t]hose in Holy Orders or with a special canonical mission."[2]

> [I]n [the liturgy] full public worship is performed by the Mystical Body of Jesus Christ, that is, by the Head and his members.
>
> From this it follows that every liturgical celebration, because it is an action of Christ the Priest and of his Body, which is the Church, is a sacred action surpassing all others. No other action of the Church can match its efficacy by the same title and to the same degree (SC 7).

---

[1] *General Instruction of the Liturgy of the Hours*, no. 27.
[2] *Ibid.*, no. 23.

Private devotions are prayers offered in one's own name. They are not part of the public liturgy of the Church and thus do not require official representation. The Rosary is a good example of a private devotion. Even when prayed in large groups, or in churches, the Rosary is not a public prayer of the Church.

As a general rule, private devotions should not be mixed within the liturgies of the Church. Doing so can confuse, remove, or diminish the value of the signs found in the public liturgies. This mixing can also confuse or diminish the roles of those present. For example, there is nothing wrong with praying a Rosary before or after Mass. There is nothing wrong with the laity gathering, even in a church, to read Sacred Scripture and encouraging one another in the spiritual life. However, the Rosary should not be prayed during the celebration of Mass. Doing so shifts the focus of the one praying away from the actions of the Mass. Likewise, having a member of the laity regularly offer reflections after the Gospel or after Communion confuses the role of the laity with that of the ordained and disrupts the intended order of the Mass.[3]

Sign Value

The liturgies of the Church, particularly the Mass and other sacraments, are filled with signs and symbols. They pertain to the official liturgy itself. The words, vestments, gestures, postures, and sacred furnishings all contribute to the full worship offered in the liturgies. Most Catholics do not know the theological symbols and signs used. This allows for changes to occur that may seem minor but, in reality, change the meaning of a particular part of the liturgy, or disrupt the proper order of the liturgy as a whole.

For example, we can compare the Mass to a piece of music written for a ballet. The music represents the actions of the dancers. If you are familiar with the story of the ballet, you can

---

[3] The confusion of roles between the laity and the ordained can occur in many situations. Because of the confusion, eight Vatican offices issued a joint instruction to clarify the matter. Entitled *Instruction on Certain Questions Concerning the Collaboration of the Lay Faithful in the Ministry of Priests* (1997), the document is essential to read for a proper understanding of this issue.

listen to Tchaikovsky's the *Nutcracker Suite* and know the events of the story. If you do not know the story of the ballet, the music may be pretty, but it has less meaning. If changed or rearranged, the story changes. You would not notice the changes if you did not know the story.

The Mass and other liturgies of the Church are affected in the same way. If you do not know the symbols and theological meanings of the actions, the Mass has less meaning for you. Some changes may seem minor, but the "story" of the Mass is distorted. As a general rule, signs and symbols pertaining to the celebration of the liturgy cannot be changed. Doing so can change the meaning, confuse doctrinal understanding, or disrupt the order of the Mass.

Different Rites

Within the Catholic Church, there are numerous rites for the celebration of the divine mysteries. These represent different traditions within the Church, but they express the same truths. For example, the Roman Rite differs from the Byzantine Rite. Both are Catholic, but the celebrations differ. Within the same ritual Church, different liturgies also abound. Within the Roman Rite, various liturgies include the *Ordo Missae* of Pope Paul VI, the Indult Mass (commonly referred to as the Tridentine Mass), and the Anglican Use liturgy. The liturgies within these differing rites are governed by their own set of laws. Mixing various elements of differing rites is prohibited. Doing so violates both the rubrics of the respective rites and the ancient traditions from which they come.

We must understand that the *Ordo Missae* of Pope Paul VI is the official Mass of the Roman Rite. Any priest of the Latin Church can celebrate according to the form of this Mass. Additionally, the rubrics and instructions for this Mass allow for certain legitimate variations. For example, the rite of blessing and sprinkling with holy water may be used in place of the penitential rite at the beginning of Mass on Sundays. Also, the Liturgy of the Hours may be merged with the celebration of Mass. If this occurs, the first part of the Liturgy of the Hours replaces the penitential rite of Mass. Furthermore, conferences of bishops may propose additional adaptations for their regions.

If approved by Rome, these adaptations become liturgical law within their region. For example, in 1969 and again in 1995, the National Conference of Catholic Bishops proposed a change requiring the faithful to "kneel beginning after the *Sanctus* [Holy, Holy, Holy] until after the Amen of the Eucharistic Prayer, that is, before the Lord's Prayer."[4] Rome approved the request both times. Consequently, the faithful in the United States must kneel during this time, but in other countries they are to stand, except at the consecration itself, when they are required to kneel.

Customs

It is important to note that certain customs which are not contrary to the rubrics and do not violate the order of Mass may arise from place to place. When considering customs as variations to the liturgy, one must keep in mind three points. First, customs arise from the spontaneous act of the people. They are not imposed as a required action by higher authority. Second, customs can be suppressed by higher authority. Finally, legitimate customs never violate the intended order of a liturgy or suggest a different interpretation of a liturgical act.

One such example is kneeling after the *Agnus Dei* (Lamb of God) during the *Ordo Missae*. Kneeling at this time is not required in the rubrics, but it also does not suggest any different interpretation of the actions of the Mass, nor does it break the intended order of the liturgy.

Lex Orandi, Lex Credendi

Our life of worship cannot be separated from our life of faith. Our worship is a profession of faith. The liturgies of the Church express the true worship of the People of God, the Body of Christ. Changes in the liturgy reflect a change in faith or a change in the understanding of faith. Mother Church takes this very seriously. To protect the liturgies from abuse, she has decreed:

---

[4] *Appendix to the General Instruction for the Dioceses of the United States of America* (1969), no. 21.

1. Regulation of the sacred liturgy depends solely on the authority of the Church, that is, on the Apostolic See, and, as laws may determine, on the bishop.

2. In virtue of power conceded by law, the regulation of the liturgy within certain defined limits belongs also to various kinds of bishops' conferences, legitimately established, with competence in given territories.

3. Therefore no other person, not even a priest, may add, remove, or change anything in the liturgy on his own authority (SC 22).

This directive has been repeated by various congregations of the Roman Curia as well as by the Pope in numerous documents since the implementation of *Sacrosanctum Concilium*.[5] Most noteworthy are the following:

The faithful have a right to a true Liturgy, which means the Liturgy desired and laid down by the Church, which has in fact indicated where adaptations may be made as called for by pastoral requirements in different places, or by different groups of people. Undue experimentation, changes and creativity bewilder the faithful. The use of unauthorized texts means a loss of the necessary connection between the *lex orandi* [law of praying] and the *lex credendi* [law of believing]. The Second Vatican Council's admonition in this regard must be remembered: "No person, even if he be a priest, may add, remove or change anything in the liturgy on his own authority." And Paul VI of venerable memory stated that:

---

[5] See the following Vatican documents: Sacred Congregation of Rites, *Instruction on the Worship of the Eucharistic Mystery* (*Eucharisticum Mysterium*, 1967); Sacred Congregation of Rites, *Second Instruction on the Proper Implementation of the Constitution on the Sacred Liturgy* (*Tres Abhinc Annos*, 1967); Sacred Congregation of Divine Worship, *Third Instruction on the Correct Application of the Constitution on the Sacred Liturgy* (*Liturgiae Instaurationes*, 1970). All of the above are found in Austin Flannery, O.P., ed., *Vatican II: The Conciliar and Post Conciliar Documents* (Northport, NY: Costello Publishing Co., 1975).

"Anyone who takes advantage of the reform to indulge in arbitrary experiments is wasting energy and offending the ecclesial sense."[6]

Following this directive, canon 846 §1 of the Code of Canon Law states: "The liturgical books approved by the competent authority are to be faithfully observed in the celebration of the sacraments; therefore no one on personal authority may add, remove or change anything in them."

In his 1988 apostolic letter *On the 25th Anniversary of the Constitution on the Sacred Liturgy*, Pope John Paul II stated:

Side by side with these benefits of the liturgical reform, one has to acknowledge with regret deviations of greater or lesser seriousness in its application. On occasion there have been noted illicit omissions or additions; rites invented outside the framework of established norms; postures or songs which are not conducive to faith or to a sense of the sacred; abuses in the practice of general absolution; confusion between the ministerial priesthood, linked with Ordination, and the common priesthood of the faithful, which has its foundation in Baptism (no. 13).

In his letter *The Mystery and Worship of the Eucharist* (*Dominicae Cenae*, 1980), Pope John Paul II further explains:

The priest as minister, as celebrant, as the one who presides over the eucharistic assembly of the faithful, should have a special *sense of the common good of the Church*, which he represents through his ministry, but to which he must also be subordinate, according to a correct discipline of faith. He cannot consider himself a "proprietor" who can make free use of the liturgical text and of the sacred rite as if it were his own property, in such a way as to stamp it with his own arbitrary personal style. At times this latter might seem more effective,

---

[6] Sacred Congregation for the Sacraments and Divine Worship, *Instruction Concerning Worship of the Eucharistic Mystery* (*Inaestimabile Donum*, 1980), foreword.

and it may better correspond to subjective piety; nevertheless, objectively it is always a betrayal of that union which should find its proper expression in the sacrament of unity.

Every priest who offers the holy Sacrifice should recall that during this Sacrifice it is not *only* he with his community that is praying but the whole Church, which is thus expressing in this sacrament her spiritual unity, among other ways by the use of the approved liturgical text. To call this position "mere insistence on uniformity" would only show ignorance of the objective requirements of authentic unity, and would be a symptom of harmful individualism (no. 12, original emphasis).

Because the Mass is the greatest prayer of the Church, the Magisterium expressly prohibits any changes contrary to the rubrics of the Mass. Yet the Church does not impose rigid uniformity on inessential matters:

It is also up to the priest in the exercise of his office of presiding over the assembly to pronounce the instructions and words of introduction and conclusion that are provided in the rites themselves. *By their very nature these introductions do not need to be expressed verbatim in the form in which they are given in the Missal; at least in certain cases it will be advisable to adapt them somewhat to the concrete situation of the community.* It also belongs to the priest presiding to proclaim the word of God and to give the final blessing. He may give the faithful a *very brief introduction* to the Mass of the day (before the celebration begins), to the liturgy of the word (before the readings), and to the eucharistic prayer (before the preface); he may also make comments concluding the entire sacred service before the dismissal.[7]

However, the central texts of the Mass must indeed be expressed verbatim in the form in which they are given in the Missal. Variations in this form are only allowed if permitted by

---

[7] GIRM, no. 11, emphasis added.

liturgical law. The translations of these prayers approved by the bishops of the region and by the Vatican are the only ones that may be used at Mass or other liturgies. The frequent repetition of such prohibitions appears to reflect widespread disregard for the approved form of the Mass.

Principles of Law

It is not uncommon that people raise concern over the actions of laity during a liturgical celebration. For the most part, laity are not official representatives of the Church during liturgical celebrations. To act as such requires appointment to a particular task by competent authority or by delegation:

> [T]he nonordained faithful do not enjoy a right to such tasks and functions. Rather, they are "capable of being admitted by the sacred pastors . . . to those functions which, in accordance with the provisions of law, they can discharge" or where "ministers are not available . . . they can supply certain of their functions . . . in accordance with the provisions of law."[8]

Common questions include: May an extraordinary minister of the Eucharist repose the Blessed Sacrament after Communion? May an extraordinary minister give a blessing to children and others in the Communion line who will not receive Communion? May an extraordinary minister preach during a Communion service?

In 1298, Pope Boniface VIII gave us the *Rules of Law*, which are still used to interpret the laws of the Church. One such rule is "He who may do the greater may do the lesser." Canon 138 of the Code of Canon Law adds the following norm: "[A] person who has received delegated power is understood to have also been granted whatever is necessary to exercise that power." With these principles in mind, we must be careful not to judge that a person in these circumstances has acted wrongly.

---

[8] *Instruction on Certain Questions Concerning the Collaboration of the Lay Faithful in the Ministry of Priests*, as published in *Origins* (November 27, 1997), vol. 27, 402, footnote omitted.

Distributing the Blessed Sacrament during Communion is arguably "more" than reposing the Blessed Sacrament afterwards. Blessings given by laity during Communion are allowed, provided certain norms are followed. Lay preaching during a Communion service is not considered a homily and is allowable, particularly if the person has a mandate from the bishop to preach. Applying these principles and determining the extent of a person's appointment or delegation can help us avoid unnecessary confrontations.

Recommendations

Whatever the causes, abuses occur in the liturgies of the Church in North America, particularly during Mass. A most important step in addressing liturgical abuses is gaining knowledge of the liturgical actions, symbols, and norms that govern the liturgies. Obtaining copies of the documents cited above is helpful. Appendix I provides a list of titles that also would be most helpful to obtain and read. Some documents are readily available in the parish. For example, the GIRM is found at the beginning of every *Sacramentary*.[9] The *Sacramentary* also contains the rubrics (rules) for Mass. Certain norms governing Mass readings are found in the front of the *Lectionary*. Information can also be obtained by contacting the National Conference of Catholic Bishops' Committee on the Liturgy.

When an act appears to be an abuse, there are several things that you can do to address it. First, pray. Offer your suffering for the sake of the Church. Consider the act in relation to the norms found in the liturgical documents. If they apply, consider the principles of law. If it is not a clear abuse of the rubrics, charitably inquire about the matter, including the extent of a person's mandate if the one acting is not a priest.

---

[9] Also known as the *Roman Missal*, this liturgical book contains the Order of the Mass. Because the GIRM has been modified since its first publication, older versions of the *Sacramentary* may not have the updated norms. It is necessary to check the date of printing prior to purchase to ensure one has the most recent edition of the GIRM before one can determine if a particular liturgical act violates the norms.

If you determine that the matter is a problem, you must also determine if it is worth addressing. For example, a priest's making announcements after the homily is a violation of GIRM, nos. 123 and 139. However, this may be considered a custom in many places and, of itself, does not constitute a serious violation of the norms. On the other hand, changing the Eucharistic Prayer, even if the words of consecration remain unchanged, is a serious violation.[10]

If the matter is worth addressing, we must make sure that our *orthodoxy* (right belief and discipline) is accompanied by *orthopraxy* (right action). In other words, we need to cultivate and use the virtues that right faith avails us—virtues such as patience, fortitude, and, above all, charity. Orthodoxy requires us to promote the truth, but never allows us to offend against charity. As the Church teaches, "[O]ne who does not . . . persevere in charity is not saved" (LG 14; cf. Catechism, no. 837). Resist the desire to speak uncharitably toward lawful authority (cf. Ex. 16:2-12; Num. 16). We should look for an opportunity to express our concerns in a manner that respects both the person and the office of a pastor. If he will not listen, approach higher authority according to the recommendations provided in Appendix II of this book.

Most importantly, we must strive never to lose faith (Sir. 2). In your frustrations, remain close to Christ in the sacraments. He remains present in the sacraments, even in our negligence or absence. Read the lives of the saints. They offer us heroic examples of patience in the face of adversity. It is this genuine fidelity to Christ and His Church that is most effective in fostering authentic liturgical renewal.

---

[10] John Paul II, *On the 25th Anniversary of the Constitution of the Sacred Liturgy*, no. 13.

Questions for Reflection
or Group Discussion

1. How do I respond when I witness an unauthorized change in the way Mass is celebrated? Am I distracted? Frustrated? Distressed? Combative?

2. Vatican II teaches that the liturgy is the "source and summit" of the Church's activity (SC 10). Do I attend Mass as a critic or do I offer any imperfections or abuses as a suffering in union with Our Eucharistic Lord, for the glory of God and the salvation of the world?

3. Read Appendix II. How can I constructively address liturgical problems in my own parish or diocese? How can I express my concerns without showing disrespect to my pastor?

COME, WORSHIP THE LORD!
Promoting Adoration of the Most Holy Eucharist

What is adoration of the Most Holy Eucharist? How can I pro-mote adoration of the Most Holy Eucharist with exposition in my parish and diocese?

The Most Holy Eucharist is the body and blood of Our Lord and Savior Jesus Christ (cf. Mt. 26:26-28; Jn. 6:55). Because this sacrament is the fullness and substance of His divinity and humanity, His presence demands proper adoration. When we adore the Most Holy Eucharist, we fulfill the first commandment, to worship only God in the fullness of our love (cf. 1 Cor. 10:14-17). Indeed, adoration of the Most Holy Eucharist is true worship in Spirit and in truth (Jn. 4:23).

The Tradition of Adoration
In general, adoration of the Blessed Sacrament occurs both during the celebration of Mass and outside of Mass. Without a doubt, the liturgy of the Mass is the greatest act of worship we offer Our Lord here on earth. This celebration expresses the fullness of our faith and gives us a foretaste of heaven's glory. During our time outside of Mass, we must continually move our hearts and minds in prayer to Our Lord. Adoration of the Most Holy Eucharist outside of Mass helps us focus our prayers on Jesus Christ, who is the Blessed Sacrament, and leads us to the Eucharistic sacrifice, which "is the summit and the source of all Christian worship and life" (canon 897).

Outside of Mass, adoration of the Most Holy Eucharist occurs whenever we worship and offer prayers to God in the presence of the Blessed Sacrament. Adoration of the Blessed Sacrament outside of Mass is strongly encouraged. For example, canon 937 provides:

Unless a grave reason prevents it, the church in which the Most Holy Eucharist is reserved should be open to the faithful for at least some hours each day so that they are able to spend time in prayer before the Most Blessed Sacrament.

Adoration of the Most Holy Eucharist outside of Mass has taken many forms throughout the history of the Church. In the early centuries of the Church, there is record that some of the faithful reserved the Blessed Sacrament within their homes privately.[1] Because the Blessed Sacrament was reserved by the priest or deacon for the sick and dying, these "private reservations" were probably for veneration, and not for reception by the sick and dying. As Pope Paul VI noted in *Mysterium Fidei*:

> The Catholic Church has always offered and still offers the cult of latria to the Sacrament of the Eucharist, not only during Mass, but also outside of it, reserving Consecrated Hosts with the utmost care, exposing them to solemn veneration, and carrying them processionally to the joy of great crowds of the faithful.

> In the ancient documents of the Church, we have many testimonies of this veneration (MF 56).

By the thirteenth century, a well-developed practice of adoring Christ in the Eucharist had developed within the Church. Recognizing the importance of such devotion to combat heresies and spiritual deprivation within society, Clement VIII issued a decree on November 25, 1592, in which he

> [established] in the city of Rome an uninterrupted course of prayer by the observation in the different churches of the devotion of the Forty Hours in such an order that at every hour of the day and night, the whole year round, the incense of prayer would ascend without interruption before the face of the Lord.[2]

---

[1] Very Rev. H.A. Ayrinhac, D.C.L., *Administrative Legislation in the New Code of Canon Law* (New York: Longman's, Green and Co., 1930), vol. 3, 132-36.
[2] Decree of Clement VIII, *Graves et Diuturnae*, as quoted in Ayrinhac, 150.

Subsequent popes continued this important work of prayer, which has continued up to this century in the city of Rome. Furthermore, on August 20, 1885, Pope Leo XIII "ordered the solemn exposition and benediction of the Blessed Sacrament every day of October as part of the Rosary devotions when held in the evening in all parish churches."[3]

The 1917 Code of Canon Law distinguished between different forms of adoration, and encouraged them all to varying degrees. For example, "private exposition" referred to the use of a ciborium during exposition. In this form of adoration, the tabernacle is opened and the ciborium moved forward while remaining in the tabernacle. This form of adoration did not require permission and was allowed in any place the Blessed Sacrament was reserved.[4]

"Public exposition" refers to the exposition of the Blessed Sacrament within a monstrance in full view of the faithful. Canon 1274 §2 of the 1917 Code of Canon Law allowed this form of adoration without permission on the Feast of Corpus Christi and every day within its octave. Public exposition during other times could occur for a just cause with the permission of the local ordinary. Furthermore, the decree of Pope Leo XIII noted above remained in force under the 1917 legislation. Finally, canon 1275 of the 1917 Code prescribed that the Forty Hours devotion was to be held in all places where the Blessed Sacrament was habitually reserved, particularly in parishes. The local ordinary was to determine the dates. If a place had too few faithful to maintain forty continuous hours of adoration, the obligation was adapted to allow some public exposition every day for three days. It seems the Church intended for each diocese what Clement VIII intended for the city of Rome.

By the time Pope Paul VI was elected to the See of Peter, continuous exposition beyond forty hours had become customary in certain places. This is commonly known as *perpetual adoration*. To protect the Blessed Sacrament from abuse and encourage this type of adoration, the Vatican Congregation of Rites

---

[3] Ayrinhac, 147.
[4] 1917 Code of Canon Law, canon 1274 §1.

promulgated the 1967 instruction *Eucharisticum Mysterium*. This document was cited and reaffirmed in the subsequent 1973 instruction *Eucharistiae Sacramentum*, issued by the Congregation for Divine Worship. Both documents follow the general legislation of the 1917 Code and encourage adoration of the Blessed Sacrament in varying forms. These norms and directives became the substance of the 1983 Code of Canon Law and the liturgical legislation that has emerged since the new Code was promulgated. In addressing "continuous" or perpetual adoration, *Eucharistiae Sacramentum* notes two possibilities: adoration initiated by the faithful, and adoration initiated by the local bishop in which the faithful are ordered to participate. Regarding adoration initiated by the faithful, the instruction provides:

> In churches where the eucharist is regularly reserved, it is recommended that solemn exposition of the blessed sacrament for an extended period of time should take place once a year, even though this period is not strictly continuous. In this way the local community may meditate on this mystery more deeply and adore.

> This kind of exposition, however, may take place with the consent of the local Ordinary, only if there is assurance of the participation of a reasonable number of the faithful (no. 86).

By "reasonable number of the faithful," the Church expects that the Blessed Sacrament will not be left unattended if exposed.

Regarding exposition ordered by the local bishop, *Eucharistiae Sacramentum* states:

> For any serious and general need, the local Ordinary is empowered to order prayer before the blessed sacrament exposed for a more extended period of time in those churches to which the faithful come in large numbers (no. 87).

The term "serious and general need" refers to the determination by the local bishop that a particularly grave situation in his diocese requires the prayerful intervention by all. Clement VIII saw the need to protect the See of Rome from spiritual attacks by ordering Forty Hours devotions held in such a way that exposition was continuous.

A bishop today can do the same in his diocese for similar reasons. For example, some bishops in the United States are addressing their priest shortage by encouraging Eucharistic exposition and adoration in their dioceses and ordering it to be held in the cathedral church. They specifically request that these prayers be offered for vocations. By "larger numbers," the instruction envisions the bishop's ordering such adoration in large parishes only, lest his decree become a burden for the faithful in smaller parishes.

In short, if the faithful wish to have Eucharistic exposition and adoration, their desire to worship and adore is reason enough, assuming adequate participation. On the other hand, if the bishop were to order the faithful to participate in public, continuous exposition of the Blessed Sacrament, he would have to have a serious reason, and should only make the demand on the larger parishes. In both instances, flexibility is provided if adequate numbers are not available. This flexibility is intended to encourage continuous exposition and adoration of the Blessed Sacrament. As *Eucharistiae Sacramentum* notes:

> Where there cannot be uninterrupted exposition because there is not a sufficient number of worshipers, it is permissible to replace the [B]lessed [S]acrament in the tabernacle at fixed hours that are announced ahead of time. But this may not be done more than twice a day, for example, at midday and at night (no. 88).

Eucharisticum Mysterium also encourages Eucharistic congresses. In these gatherings, the faithful seek to understand more deeply the meaning and purpose of the Blessed Sacrament. They offer prayers and participate in devotions and processions. All they do is directed to the celebration of Mass and presence of Christ in the Eucharist. As the instruction notes, "All during a [E]ucharistic congress of at least an entire region, it is proper to designate some churches for continuous adoration" (no. 67). Both Paul VI and John Paul II have attended many of the international Eucharistic congresses and encouraged the faithful to continue this important act of worship.

Promotion of Eucharistic Exposition

Pope John Paul II has strongly encouraged veneration of the Blessed Sacrament through Eucharistic exposition and adoration. As he stated during the forty-fifth International Eucharistic Congress in Spain,

> In fact, the *continual adoration*—which took place in many churches throughout the city, and in some even at night—was an enriching feature that distinguished this Congress. If only this form of adoration, which ends tonight in a solemn Eucharistic vigil, would continue in the future too, so that in all the parishes and Christian communities the custom of some form of adoration of the Eucharist might take root.[5]

Following the encouragement of our Holy Father, we can do several things to foster Eucharistic adoration, particularly exposition. We should worship the Most Holy Eucharist at every opportunity. At the very least, opportunity exists every time we pass a church in which the Blessed Sacrament is reserved. Saint Philip Neri could not pass a church without stopping for a visit and, if locked, he would pray at the door. Because of his efforts, Forty Hours devotion spread through the parishes in Rome, even before the decree of Clement VIII. Following the example of so great a saint, we could express our intimate love for Our Eucharistic Lord by making an ejaculatory prayer with the Sign of the Cross every time we pass a church. Such acts keep us focused on our Eucharistic Lord and make us docile to the promptings of the Holy Spirit.

If exposition of the Blessed Sacrament does not occur regularly in your parish, approach the pastor and request it. First, spend some time every day for thirty days in adoration before the Blessed Sacrament. Become accustomed to scheduled visits. Meditate on His Real Presence. Study the documents of the

---

[5] Address to the 45th International Eucharistic Congress in Spain, no. 2; *L'Osservatore Romano* (English ed., June 23, 1993), 4, original emphasis.

Church that discuss this subject. In this way, you will be prepared both spiritually and mentally to approach your pastor, answer his questions, and accept his decisions.

We must be docile to the decision of our bishop concerning Eucharistic exposition:

> The bishop is responsible for all matters pertaining to the right ordering of the celebration of the Eucharist and adoration and devotion to the Eucharist outside Mass. It is his duty to promote and guide the liturgical life of the diocese. Consequently, he alone determines the pastoral appropriateness of perpetual exposition in his diocese and accordingly may permit it or not and may limit the number of places where it takes place.[6]

If exposition already occurs in your parish or a neighboring parish, become involved. If already involved, try to arouse interest in having a local Eucharistic congress. This will help spread the word about Eucharistic exposition and increase devotion to the Blessed Sacrament.

Most importantly, do not neglect to attend Mass. Attendance during the week, if possible, is a most important way to adore Our Lord and encourage devotion to the Blessed Sacrament. All our prayers and devotions must be directed to this greatest of prayers. As Pope Paul VI exhorts us in *Mysterium Fidei*:

> It is to be desired that the faithful, every day and in great numbers, actively participate in the Sacrifice of the Mass, receive Holy Communion with a pure heart, and give thanks to Christ Our Lord for so great a gift. Let them remember these words: "The desire of Jesus Christ and of the Church that all the faithful receive daily Communion means above all that through the sacramental union with God they may obtain the strength necessary for mastering their passions, for purifying themselves of their daily venial faults and for avoiding the grave sins to which human frailty is exposed" (MF 66).

---

[6] "Perpetual Exposition of the Blessed Sacrament," Newsletter of the U.S. Bishops' Committee on the Liturgy (June 1995), vol. xxi, 22.

Questions for Reflection
or Group Discussion

1. Am I generous with my time when it comes to prayer before the Blessed Sacrament?

2. Vatican II teaches that the sacred liturgy is the source and summit of the Christian life. How do I understand and put into practice this teaching? What role does Eucharistic adoration outside Mass have in living out this teaching?

3. Is Eucharistic adoration with exposition available in my area? Do I take advantage of this opportunity? What can I do to foster the spread of Eucharistic adoration?

Chapter 6

THE GOSPEL TRUTH CONCERNING LAY READERS
The Role of the Laity During the Liturgy of the Word

May a lay person proclaim all the readings at Mass?

Father, you teach us in both the Old and the New Testament to celebrate this passover mystery. Help us to understand your great love for us. May the goodness you now show us confirm our hope in your future mercy. We ask this through Christ our Lord. Amen.[1]

This prayer expresses the Church's intention to teach us the mysteries of our faith through the Liturgy of the Word so we might worthily participate in the Mass. Within the Liturgy of the Word, ministers read the writings of Sacred Scripture aloud, and a priest or deacon preaches a homily intended to aid the faithful in understanding the readings they have just heard.

The Church carefully selects readings to correspond to the different cycles of the Church year. In Advent, we hear readings that express hope in the promised coming of the Messiah. During Lent, we hear readings that encourage us to remain faithful in our discipline of penance. During Ordinary Time, the revelation of salvation history unfolds within the readings each week. In this way, those who attend Mass daily hear the most important passages in the Bible read in two years, while Sunday readings cover much of the Bible in three years. Thus, the readings properly root our spiritual lives in Sacred Scripture. Furthermore, they introduce the theme of the celebration, turn our minds to truth, and enliven our hearts to enter the Liturgy of the Eucharist with humility and true devotion.

---

[1] Alternate prayer after the seventh reading during Easter Vigil, as found in the *Sacramentary* (New York: Catholic Book Publishing Co., 1985), 191.

Lectors and Readers

Because of the importance of the Liturgy of the Word in the formation of the faithful, specific laws determine who may read. Only those who have received Holy Orders—a deacon, priest, or bishop—may proclaim the Gospel. As a rule a deacon or, in his absence, a priest other than the celebrant, should read the Gospel at Mass. If there is no deacon or another priest present, the celebrant himself should proclaim the Gospel (GIRM, nos. 34, 66). However, in certain circumstances, lay people may proclaim the Gospel at children's Masses.[2]

Regarding the other readings and the responsorial psalm, only a person properly instituted for the purpose of reading during Mass should read them. The Church first prefers a man installed into the ministry of lector to read the readings. In the absence of such a man, other laity, women included, who have received proper training and authorization as a reader may read. In the absence of either, anyone who meets the requirements established by the local bishop can be asked to read. If no one is available, the priest or deacon must read the readings.

As noted in canon 230 §1, "Lay men who possess the age and qualifications determined by decree of the conference of bishops can be installed on a stable basis in the minist[ry] of lector." The use of the word "*vir*" in the original Latin precludes women from participating in "the stable ministry" of lector. However, paragraph two of this same canon notes that "[l]ay persons can fulfill the function of lector during liturgical actions by temporary deputation." According to canon 230 and liturgical law, in the absence of a man installed into the stable ministry of lector, a man or woman can be authorized to act as reader during the celebration of Mass.

---

[2] See CUF FAITH FACT, "Children's Masses: May Lay People Read the Gospel and Give the Homily?"

Opening Minds and Hearts to Christ

The Vatican II document *Sacrosanctum Concilium* notes that those who act as lector or reader "should carry out all and only those parts [of the Mass] which pertain to his office by the nature of the rite and the norms of the liturgy" (SC 28). It further notes, "[T]hey must be deeply imbued with the spirit of the liturgy, each in his own measure, and they must be trained to perform their functions in a correct and orderly manner" (SC 29). It is the responsibility of the local bishop to provide the norms for the formation and training of lectors and readers in his diocese. The selection process should ensure that those who participate in this ministry are examples of faith and charity within the community. Further, their training should prepare them to proclaim the Word of God in a manner that moves the minds and hearts of the congregation to Christ (cf. GIRM, no. 66).

Regarding the exercise of this ministry during Mass, the liturgical books emphasize three important points. First, on Sundays and solemnities, when two readings and the psalm are provided, it is permissible to distribute the readings between different readers.[3] This does not mean two lectors can read portions of the same reading, but rather each is given a reading to present to the faithful in its entirety.

Second, if seated in the congregation during Mass, a lector should genuflect if he passes before the tabernacle when entering the sanctuary to read, because "a genuflection is made before and after Mass and whenever anyone passes in front of the [B]lessed [S]acrament" (GIRM, no. 233). This gesture offers proper reverence to the physical presence of the Word of God, the "living bread" given for the life of the world (Jn. 6:51).

Third, the nature of the Mass demands the active participation of all the faithful (SC 14). For some, this participation includes serving as a lector or reader. Traditionally, the Church has not reserved this ministry to the celebrant. For this reason, the GIRM notes that "the reader has his own

---

[3] Cf. Sacred Congregation for Divine Worship, *Lectionary for Mass* (1969), nos. 51-55.

proper function in the eucharistic celebration, and should exercise this even though ministers of a higher rank may be present" (no. 66). This means that although a deacon, or even another priest, is present, such ministers have a function separate from that of lector and their presence does not require the reader or lector to relinquish his role.[4]

God's Word Is Living and Active (Heb. 4:12)

The Church encourages all Catholics to read the Bible frequently and prayerfully. Vatican II "forcefully and specifically exhorts all the Christian faithful . . . to learn 'the surpassing knowledge of Jesus Christ' (Phil. 3:8) by frequent reading of the divine Scriptures" (DV 25; cf. Catechism, nos. 133, 2653). This assuredly prepares the faithful for the Liturgy of the Word at Mass, when "God speaks to his people" (SC 33) before revealing Himself "in the breaking of the bread" (Lk. 24:35).

Some members of the lay faithful are able to make important contributions to the celebration of Mass during the Liturgy of the Word. Their active participation should reflect the mind of Christ. When fulfilling their roles as lectors or readers, they should know that the faithful present are hearing Christ. They should bear in mind the words of Saint John the Baptist, "He must increase, but I must decrease" (Jn. 3:30). In this way, they will truly fulfill their task of turning the minds of the faithful to Christ and enlivening their hearts to receive Him reverently in the Eucharist.

---

[4] In contrast, an extraordinary minister of the Eucharist is expected to relinquish his role to an ordinary minister, namely a bishop, priest, or deacon. Cf. 1997 Vatican document, *Instruction on Certain Questions Concerning the Collaboration of the Lay Faithful in the Ministry of Priests*, art. 8. For further discussion of this topic, see CUF's FAITH FACT, "Ordinary and Extraordinary Eucharistic Ministers."

Questions for Reflection
or Group Discussion

1. Do I read Sacred Scripture daily? What can I do to increase my knowledge of the Word of God?

2. What qualities make for an effective lector or reader?

3. How do I understand the role of the lector, deacon, priest, or bishop in proclaiming and explaining the Word of God?

SPIRITUAL PARENTS
The Role of Godparents in the Catholic Church

What is the role of godparents (sponsors)? What are the Catholic Church's norms regarding godparents? May a Catholic serve as a godparent for a non-Catholic? May a non-Catholic Christian serve as a godparent for a Catholic? Finally, may a Catholic have more than one godfather and godmother?

To understand the role of godparents, we must first understand the purpose and effects of Baptism and Confirmation. In addition to the forgiveness of all sins (cf. Catechism, no. 1263) and the placement of an indelible mark on the person's soul (cf. Catechism, nos. 1272-74), Baptism has two other effects that are social in nature: The person becomes an adopted son of God (cf. Catechism, no. 1265), and he becomes a member of the Body of Christ, which is the Church (cf. Catechism, nos. 1267-71).

Confirmation completes Baptism (cf. Catechism, nos. 1303-04). Because it completes Baptism, the social effects of Confirmation are similar to those of Baptism. The person is conformed more perfectly to Christ as a son of God, is more perfectly united to the Body of Christ, and is strengthened to bear witness to the faith in daily life. The godparents' role is directly related to these social effects of Baptism and Confirmation.

When a person receives Baptism, God forgives his sins and removes all punishment due to sin. The Father grants him the gift of salvation. However, he can lose this gift. Just as the king expected his servants to use their talents for his glory and took away the talents from the unworthy servant (Lk. 19:11-27), so God expects us to work out our salvation through prayer and acts of charity. In short, we must continually conform ourselves to Christ (Phil. 1:27-2:18; Catechism, nos. 1691-96). Thus, Baptism is only the beginning of a new spiritual life, in which we must grow in virtue and grace before God and man. This growth in virtue and grace reflects our status as God's children by adoption and as members of the Church.

Examples of Faith

A godparent's role is to assist the growth of the baptized in his new spiritual life. As adopted sons of God and members of His family, the Church, the baptized must live in harmony with the Family of God. A godparent promises to provide an example of faith to "help the baptized to lead a Christian life in harmony with baptism, and to fulfill faithfully the obligations connected with it" (canon 872). If the baptized is an infant or child whose parents are faithful Catholics, the godparent assists the parents, who are the primary teachers of the faith (GE 3). If the baptized is an infant or child whose parents are not faithful to the Church, or if the baptized is an adult, the godparent must provide a primary role in the spiritual growth of his godchild.

The greatest help a godparent provides is an example of faith. The godparent must foster the virtues within himself and provide an example of prayer. As part of this example of faith, the godparent must be involved in the life of his godchild. No one is an example unless he is seen by those to whom he witnesses. Being actively involved in the life of a godchild fosters a strong relationship and enables the godparent to serve as a role model. The godchild can then better understand his status as a child of God.

Special Requirements

Because this role is so important, a godparent in the Catholic Church must (1) be a Catholic in full communion with the Church; (2) be properly designated and accept the responsibilities; (3) meet age requirements recognized in the diocese where the Baptism takes place; and (4) not be the mother or father of the one baptized (GE 3; canon 874 §1). A godparent cannot provide an example of faith if he does not share the faith. Because a godparent promises to assist in the formation of the newly baptized, and agrees to represent the community of faith and encourage his godchild to remain in full communion with the Church, he must be in full communion with the Catholic Church himself. That is, a godparent for a Catholic must be a

Catholic in good standing. He must have received Holy Communion and the Sacrament of Confirmation, and he must be living a life in harmony with the faith (GE 3; cf. canon 874). He also must be eligible to receive the sacraments and cannot be bound by any ecclesiastical penalty. Of particular concern today are Catholics married outside the Church. Because such a person is not living a life in harmony with the teachings and practice of the Church, he is not eligible to receive the Sacrament of Holy Communion. Until he reconciles himself with the Church, he may not act as a godparent.

Regarding the first requirement that a godparent be Catholic, there is one exception that concerns the relationship between Eastern Rite Catholics and our separated brethren in the Orthodox Church. "For a just cause," regarding the Baptism of an Eastern Catholic, "it is permitted to admit the Christian faithful of another Eastern non-Catholic Church to the function of a sponsor, but always at the same time with a Catholic sponsor."[1] This means that a Ukrainian Catholic may have a Russian Orthodox godparent, provided that there is a good reason for it (family relationship) and he also has another Catholic godparent.

Godparents and Witnesses

Because Baptism is the sacrament that unites all Christians (cf. Catechism, no. 1271), and because the Church recognizes the importance of family relationships and close friendships, a Catholic may serve as a "witness" for a non-Catholic in Baptism, but not as a godparent. A Catholic cannot serve as a godparent for someone who has no intention of growing in the Catholic faith. Likewise, one non-Catholic may act as a "witness" at a Catholic Baptism, but only if a Catholic is also acting as godparent for the baptized.[2] These pastoral norms allow family relationships to be fostered and the faith to be witnessed to non-Catholics.

---

[1] *Code of Canons of the Eastern Churches*, *Latin-English Edition* (Washington: Canon Law Society of America, 1990), canon 685 §5.

[2] Pontifical Council for Promoting Christian Unity, *The 1993 Directory for Ecumenism*, no. 98; cf. canon 874 §2.

As noted above, it is necessary that the godparents be chosen for that purpose and accept the responsibilities. The godparents must also meet any requirements set forth by the local bishop. These requirements are meant to ensure that the godparent takes the responsibilities seriously and is able to fulfill them.

The godparents must not be the parents of the baptized. According to the Church's ancient tradition, a spiritual relationship arises between the godparent and the one baptized. This relationship establishes a bond in faith and carries responsibilities of spiritual parenthood. If a child's natural parents do not raise and form the person in the faith, godparents must fulfill this obligation. Parents already have a parental relationship that is primary and, if they were the godparents, there would be no one designated to assist them or take their place in their absence. This spiritual relationship is so strong that, in former days, the Church would not allow a godparent and godchild to marry. While this prohibition to marriage no longer exists in the Western Church, it does exist in the Eastern Catholic Churches. This means that in the Eastern Catholic Churches, one may not serve as the godparent of a prospective spouse, although this may be dispensed by the local bishop.[3] Furthermore, this spiritual relationship is so important that the Church recommends that "the one who undertook the role of sponsor (godparent) at baptism be sponsor for confirmation" (canon 893 §2).

Finally, for a Catholic baptismal candidate, "one sponsor, male or female is sufficient; but there may be two, one of each sex" (canon 873). Therefore, Catholics can only have one godfather, one godmother, or one of each.

Building the Family of God

Being a godparent is an important duty in the Catholic Church. Often, godparents are chosen from family members and close friends. Quite often, godparents do not live in the same locale as their godchild. While this makes it difficult to be a part of the child's life, it is not impossible. At the very

---

[3] Code of Canons of the Eastern Churches, canon 811 §1.

least, godparents should send cards on their godchild's Baptism day, Confirmation day, birthday, Christmas, or other significant days in his life. Remembering their Baptism and Confirmation encourages the godchild to call upon the grace received from these sacraments and live a life worthy of a child of God. They should keep in contact by letter, telephone and, if possible, personal visits. Parents should encourage the relationship between their children and their children's godparents. In this way, the children will not consider Baptism or Confirmation simply a nice thing that happens. Rather, they will experience a concrete relationship that bears witness to their status as adopted children of God. Further, they will be encouraged to live life in harmony with the greater family of the Church.

Questions for Reflection or Group Discussion

1. What is the role of a godparent (sponsor)?

2. How do I understand the Sacraments of Baptism and Confirmation? How does my understanding of these sacraments affect my relationship with my godparents?

3. What can I do to foster a proper spiritual relationship with my godparents? (For parents) What can I do to foster a proper spiritual relationship between my children and their godparents? (For godparents) What can I do to foster a proper spiritual relationship with my godchild?

GOING GOD'S WAY
The Church's Teaching on Moral Conscience

What does the Church teach concerning moral conscience?

Moral conscience is man's most secret core, and his sanctuary. It is there that "man discovers a law which he has not laid upon himself but which he must obey" (GS 16). In his conscience, man not only discovers the natural law (cf. Rom. 2:15) but encounters God Himself, the author of the law.

While the natural law written on our hearts teaches us the general, objective principles of the moral life, conscience applies the natural law to particular circumstances, enabling us to choose what is good and avoid what is evil (cf. Catechism, no. 1777).

While all of us have the right and duty to follow our consciences, it is likewise true that our consciences must be correctly formed, and that is truly a lifelong task.

In the formation of conscience, the Word of God is the light for our path (cf. Ps. 119:105); we must assimilate it in faith and prayer and put it into practice (cf. Catechism, no. 1785). Further, in forming our consciences, we must be "guided by the authoritative teaching of the Church" (*ibid.*; cf. DH 14).

One of the principal documents of Vatican II, *Gaudium et Spes*, devoted an entire paragraph (no. 16) to the subject of conscience. It is worth quoting in full:

> Deep within his conscience man discovers a law which he has not laid upon himself but which he must obey. Its voice, ever calling him to love and to do what is good and to avoid evil, tells him inwardly at the right moment: do this, shun that. For man has in his heart a law inscribed by God. His dignity lies in observing this law, and by it he will be judged

(cf. Rom. 2:15-16). His conscience is man's most secret core, and his sanctuary. There he is alone with God whose voice echoes in his depths. By conscience, in a wonderful way, that law is made known which is fulfilled in the love of God and of one's neighbor (cf. Mt. 22:37-40; Gal. 5:14). Through loyalty to conscience Christians are joined to other men in the search for truth and for the right solution to so many moral problems which arise both in the life of individuals and from social relationships. Hence, the more a correct conscience prevails, the more do persons and groups turn aside from blind choice and try to be guided by the objective standards of moral conduct. Yet it often happens that conscience goes astray through ignorance which it is unable to avoid, without thereby losing its dignity. This cannot be said of the man who takes little trouble to find out what is true and good, or when conscience is by degrees almost blinded through the habit of committing sin.

Listening to Conscience

Moral conscience, which helps us to make good choices in conformity with God's plan for our lives, is a sign of our tremendous dignity as human persons created in the image and likeness of God (cf. Gen. 1:26-27). The Catechism points out, however, that we need "interiority" (i.e., adequate reflection, self-examination, etc.) in order to hear and follow the voice of conscience amidst the many distractions in our lives (cf. Catechism, no. 1779).

Conscience enables us to take responsibility for our actions. The judgment of conscience bears witness to the fact that we have made good choices, but also convicts us when we have made bad choices (i.e., committed sins), leading us to seek forgiveness: "[W]e shall . . . reassure our hearts before him whenever our hearts condemn us; for God is greater than our hearts, and he knows everything" (1 Jn. 3:19-20).

The Church has always affirmed that we must not deliberately act against the certain judgment of our consciences (cf. Catechism, nos. 1790, 1800). Saint Bonaventure, the great thirteenth-century Franciscan scholar and doctor of the Church, put it this way:

[C]onscience is like God's herald and messenger; it does not command things on its own authority, but commands them as coming from God's authority, like a herald when he proclaims the edict of the king. This is why conscience has binding force.[1]

"If your eye is not sound . . . how great is the darkness!" (Mt. 6:23)

Yet it does not follow that every judgment of conscience is correct. "Faced with a moral choice, conscience can make either a right judgment in accordance with reason and the divine law or, on the contrary, an erroneous judgment that departs from them" (Catechism, no. 1786). As mentioned in the above quote from Vatican II, it is possible that a judgment of one's conscience may be erroneous through ignorance, and a person may not be at fault for acting on such a judgment. But even if there is no sin, the bad choice is still a disorder, and one must work to correct the errors of moral conscience (ibid., no. 1793).

Further, we are responsible for forming our consciences, allowing God's Word to truly be a light for our path. When we do not respect the dignity of conscience—when we do not seek what is true and good—the conscience becomes increasingly blind and less capable of making sound moral judgments (cf. Mt. 6:22-23; VS 63).

The Catechism (no. 1792) gives several examples of how conscience can go astray, identifying the following sources of errors of judgment in moral conduct:

• ignorance of Christ and His Gospel
• bad example of others
• enslavement to passions
• mistaken notion of autonomy of conscience
• rejection of the Church's authority and her teaching
• lack of conversion
• lack of charity

---

[1] II Librum Sentent., dist. 39, a. 1, q. 3, conclusion: Ed. Ad Claras Aquas, II, 907b, as quoted in VS 58 (Vatican translation).

Conscience is our personal link to God's law, and it must be distinguished—often with the help of a confessor or spiritual director—from our natural inclinations and "passions." And deep down we know that as Catholics we are not acting with a "certain" conscience when we make choices known to be at odds with the Church's moral teaching.

It is interesting to note that in discussing the "culture of death" in his encyclical *Evangelium Vitae* (The Gospel of Life), Pope John Paul II also speaks, in an analogous sense, of the "moral conscience of society" (nos. 21-24). He speaks of the eclipse of the sense of God in our society and further teaches that, "when the sense of God is lost, there is also a tendency to lose the sense of man" (no. 21). In the area of human life issues such as contraception, abortion, suffering, poverty, euthanasia, etc., we witness on a societal level what happens to an individual who routinely ignores the truth of God and the truth of man: The distinction between good and evil is blurred, and eventually one may call "evil good and good evil" (Is. 5:20).

Yet, even in the case of extreme moral corruption on an individual or societal level, the voice of the Lord continues to beckon us to seek reconciliation and a fresh beginning (cf. EV 24).

The Truth That Sets Us Free

Any discussion of conscience has to take truth into account. After all, Jesus came "to bear witness to the truth" (Jn. 18:37). Vatican II's *Dignitatis Humanae* (no. 8) emphasizes that the aim of religious freedom is to enable people to "form their own judgments in the light of truth."

But where is truth found? That same Vatican II declaration further provides:

> [I]n forming their consciences the faithful must pay careful attention to the sacred and certain teaching of the Church. For the Catholic Church is by the will of Christ the teacher of truth. It is her duty to proclaim and teach with authority the truth which is Christ and, at the same time, to declare and confirm by her authority the principles of the moral order which spring from human nature itself (DH 14).

Some Catholic commentators assert that a well-formed conscience and official Catholic teaching may come to opposite conclusions in moral matters. This opinion directly contradicts Catechism, no. 2039: "Personal conscience and reason should not be set in opposition to the moral law or the Magisterium of the Church." A Catholic simply cannot claim to have a well-formed and well-informed conscience if he or she is ignorant of, misunderstands, or rejects outright God's law and thus commits acts that the Church considers gravely disordered.

One who "disregards or refuses to hold as true what God has revealed and the Church proposes for belief" is "sinning against faith" (Catechism, no. 2088). Assuredly, there may be circumstances present that diminish the individual's guilt, but that is very different from saying that the conscience is well formed.

The Church is not merely one source to be consulted as we form our conscience. The Church is the Mystical Body of Christ. If we believe that Jesus is truly God, then we do not "consult" with Him—we follow Him! The Church's moral teaching is not just something that we can buy into in varying degrees based on our own personal preference. Rather, it is the truth of Jesus Christ that sets us free (cf. Jn. 8:32) and enables us to live fulfilling Christian lives.

We believe with a divine and Catholic faith all that Christ has revealed. Can we deliberately choose to reject any of Christ's teachings and still call ourselves His disciples (cf. Mt. 7:21)?

"He who does what is true comes to the light" (Jn. 3:21)

In his encyclical on the moral life, *Veritatis Splendor* (Splendor of Truth), Pope John Paul II explains that a correct conscience involves a judgment in accordance with objective truth, while an erroneous conscience involves a judgment that a person subjectively considers to be true, but is not (nos. 62-63).

A good conscience, then, must be attuned to the truth, as found not only through natural law but also through the revealed truths of Jesus Christ as taught by His Church. The education of conscience and the fostering of the virtues is absolutely necessary if we are to be "transformed by the renewal of our minds" (Rom. 12:2; cf. Catechism, nos. 1783-85; VS 64).

Scripture teaches that "to live is Christ" (Phil. 1:21). We must allow His Word to enlighten our minds and change our hearts. Then, through the grace of Christ and the gifts of His Spirit, we are empowered to lead lives "worthy of the gospel" (Phil. 1:27), making good choices in keeping with our dignity as Christians.

_____*SideBar*_____

Trust the Church

Trust the Church of God implicitly even when your natural judgment would take a different course from hers and would induce you to question her prudence or correctness. Recollect what a hard task she has; how she is sure to be criticized and spoken against, whatever she does; recollect how much she needs your loyal and tender devotion; recollect, too, how long is the experience gained in 1800 years; and what a right she has to claim your assent to principles which have had so extended and triumphant a trial. Thank her that she has kept the faith safe for so many generations and do your part in helping her to transmit it to generations after you.

—Ven. John Henry Newman (d. 1890)

Questions for Reflection
or Group Discussion

1. Catechism, no. 1792 identifies some causes of errors of judgment when it comes to living a moral, Christian life. Are any of these items present in my own life? Do I understand God's law as a source of freedom or a form of bondage? Do I live as a child of God?

2. The Church emphasizes the importance of having a properly formed conscience. What can I do to help ensure that my conscience is properly formed? (See Catechism, no. 1785.)

3. How would I charitably respond to someone who says, "I'm Catholic, but I disagree with many of the Church's moral teachings. I follow my conscience on the subject of contraception and abortion"?

Chapter 9

PERSEVERING TO THE END
The Biblical Reality of Mortal Sin

Is the distinction between mortal and venial sin biblical? Can we
"lose" our salvation by committing a mortal sin?

The Bible describes sins that are *mortal* (or "unto death"),
and those that are not mortal, which we commonly call *venial*
(cf. 1 Jn. 5:16-17; Catechism, nos. 1852-54).

Christians are capable of committing mortal sins, thereby
rejecting the gift of eternal life, a gift that cannot be taken for
granted. However, Christians who choose to persevere in
faithfulness—and seek reconciliation through the Sacrament
of Confession should they sin—may be confident in God's
infinite mercy and His fidelity to His promises.

There are two closely related questions here. First, is it
possible for a Christian to lose sanctifying grace (i.e., his
"salvation") by committing a serious sin? Second, if it is possible
for a Christian to commit such a sin, does this mean that our
salvation is in jeopardy?

We must begin by realizing that at the heart of Jesus Christ's
mission was the proclamation of good news—God's mercy to
sinners. The angel announced to Saint Joseph: "You shall call his
name Jesus, for he will save his people from their sins" (Mt. 1:21).

God's mercy is greater than our sins. "[W]here sin increased,
grace abounded all the more" (Rom. 5:20). In Luke 15, in the
parables of the lost sheep, the lost coin, and the prodigal son,
we discover the utter delight Our Heavenly Father takes in
showering His mercy on those who turn to Him for forgiveness.
Christians are called not only to experience reconciliation
with God, but to be ambassadors of reconciliation to the world
(cf. Mt. 6:14; 2 Cor. 5:18-20).

The fact that Christians may, like the prodigal son, choose
to sever their relationship with God through mortal sin

demonstrates that in making us His sons and daughters through Jesus Christ, God leaves intact our free will and thus our ability to turn away from Him.

However, He is waiting to embrace each prodigal son and daughter that turns back to Him. Further, all Christians have received the gift of the Holy Spirit to help them lead godly lives. The possibility of mortal sin, then, should not be a cause for undue anxiety or worry. Rather, it demonstrates that our choices—good and bad—matter to a God who wants us to love Him freely.

Church Teaching on Mortal Sin

The Bible makes a clear distinction between mortal and venial ("not mortal") sin in 1 John 5:16-17:

> If any one sees his brother committing what is not a mortal sin, he will ask, and God will give him life for those whose sin is not mortal. There is sin which is mortal; I do not say that one is to pray for that. All wrongdoing is sin, but there is sin which is not mortal.

Mortal sin is called "mortal" because it "kills" the life of grace in a Christian. God has freely given men His grace and will not take it back from them, but they may choose to reject this grace themselves through deliberate, grave sins. Saint James speaks of saving a brother from mortal sin (Jas. 5:19-20), and Saint Paul notes that there are sins which, if unrepented, will prevent a person from inheriting the kingdom of God (1 Cor. 6:9-10). In addition, Hebrews 10:26-36 discusses deliberate or "willful" sin:

> For if we sin deliberately after receiving the knowledge of the truth, there no longer remains a sacrifice for sins, but a fearful prospect of judgment. . . . How much worse punishment do you think will be deserved by the man who has spurned the Son of God and profaned the blood of the covenant by which he was sanctified, and outraged the Spirit of grace? . . . For you have need of endurance, so that you may do the will of God, and receive what is promised.

This passage clearly shows that those who have received Jesus, yet sin deliberately afterwards, thereby reject the sanctifying or justifying grace they have received, i.e., the grace by which they partook of God's nature (2 Pet. 1:4) and became sons and daughters of God (Rom. 8:14-17; cf. Catechism, nos. 1987-2005). In order to be reconciled with God, they need to repent and confess their sins (1 Jn. 1:9). Christians within God's grace, or restored to God's grace, must strive to persevere in that life of grace (Heb. 10:36; Rom. 11:22; 1 Cor. 10:12).

For a sin to be mortal, three conditions must be present. The sin must involve *grave matter* and be committed with *full knowledge* and *deliberate consent* (cf. Catechism, nos. 1854-64, 1874). The Catechism (no. 1858) teaches that "grave matter" is specified by the Ten Commandments, corresponding to Jesus' answer to the rich young man: "Do not kill, Do not commit adultery, Do not steal, Do not bear false witness, Do not defraud, Honor your father and your mother" (Mk. 10:19).

"Full knowledge" refers to the understanding that the act is in opposition to God's law (cf. Catechism, no. 1959). "Deliberate consent" means that the act is committed as a free choice by the person (*ibid.*). If a person does not know a particular act is a serious offense, or if he acts without sufficient freedom, the sin is not mortal.

In his 1993 encyclical letter *Veritatis Splendor* (Splendor of Truth), Pope John Paul II masterfully summarizes the Church's teaching concerning mortal sin:

With the whole tradition of the Church, we call mortal sin the act by which man freely and consciously rejects God, his law, the covenant of love that God offers, preferring to turn in on himself or to some created and finite reality, something contrary to the divine will (*conversio ad creaturam*). This can occur in a direct and formal way, in the sins of idolatry, apostasy, and atheism; or in an equivalent way, as in every act of disobedience to God's commandments in a grave matter (no. 70).

Perseverance Is Essential

Some people teach the idea "once saved, always saved." They claim that once a person has received Jesus, he can never lose his salvation. After all, since salvation can't be earned (cf. Eph. 2:8-9), how can it be lost?

Is this position biblical? No, because the Bible clearly teaches the reality of mortal sin and the need for repentance, endurance, and perseverance—remaining in God's grace and not committing mortal sin—in the life of a Christian. "Once saved, always saved" or "assurance of [final] salvation" is not biblical.

Those who teach the concept of "once saved, always saved" will sometimes quote biblical verses out of context or misinterpret verses to support their belief. Nevertheless, the biblical teaching on the need for perseverance is clear and unquestionably opposed to "once saved, always saved."

Consider the words of Peter's Second Letter:

> For it would have been better for them [who have knowledge of our Lord and Savior Jesus Christ, yet become entangled in sin] never to have known the way of righteousness than after knowing it to turn back from the holy commandment delivered to them (2:21).

In this passage, Saint Peter plainly teaches that it would be better never to know Jesus at all than to know Him and commit grave sin, meaning that the fallen-away Christian, having rejected Jesus, is in a worse place than he was originally. This falling away does not preclude the possibility of repentance and reconciliation, but the man's "fall from grace" makes no sense if his salvation was assured the moment he received Christ. For how could a man who turns away from Christ be "assured of salvation" if the Bible says he is in a worse position than when he never knew Christ at all? If a man were "always saved" from the moment he received Christ, committing grave sins would have no consequences worse than never receiving Christ; yet Sacred Scripture says that the consequences are worse.

Saint Paul discusses a similar situation in 1 Timothy 5:8: "If any one does not provide for his relatives, and especially for his own family, he has disowned the faith and is worse than an unbeliever." This verse speaks of a Christian who violates Jesus' commandment to love others (1 Jn. 2:3-4; Mt. 22:37-40). To commit such a grave sin, Saint Paul says, is to renounce the faith. As with Saint Peter, so with Saint Paul: The man who turns away from Christ is worse off than if he had never believed. Again, this could not be true if a Christian's salvation were "assured." If "once saved, always saved" were true, committing grave sin as a believer could never be worse than being an unbeliever.

Confidence in God Alone

In rejecting the idea of "once saved, always saved," we must not go to the other extreme of doubting God's mercy, goodness, and fidelity to His promises. In other words, we need the virtue of hope (cf. Catechism, nos. 1817-21).

When we were baptized, we were neither whisked away into heaven nor left to our own devices on earth. Rather, we embarked on a pilgrimage to our eternal home prepared from all eternity for us by Our Father in heaven (cf. Jn. 14:1-3; 2 Cor. 5:1-10; Phil. 3:13-14).

The Church reminds us that hope is expressed and nourished in prayer, especially in the Our Father, which summarizes the aspirations of all Christians. Prayer focuses us on our goal— God Himself—and inclines us to reject anything (i.e., sin) that would keep us from Him.

As we journey toward our eternal home, we are buoyed by the gift of the Holy Spirit, who is Christ's legacy to His Church. Our salvation requires our cooperation, but our confidence is not in our own efforts, but in God, who will never disappoint us (cf. Rom. 5:5). If we are with Christ, we will be saved (cf. 1 Jn. 5:12).

_____SideBar___

Once Saved, Always Saved?

- We must persevere "to the end" (Mt. 10:22; 24:13) "in the kindness of God" (Rom. 11:22) in order to reign with Christ (2 Tim. 2:12).

- Scripture mentions several cases of Christians who have fallen away through sin (e.g., 1 Tim. 5:8; Heb. 6:4-6; Jas. 5:19-20; 2 Pet. 2:20-21).

- Saint Paul, who had one of the most dramatic and profound conversions in 2,000 years of Christianity, writes, "I pommel my body and subdue it, lest after preaching to others I myself should be disqualified" (1 Cor. 9:27).

- Saint Paul further advises those who are already Christians to "work out your own salvation with fear and trembling" (Phil. 2:12).

- Christians are called to cultivate the theological virtue of hope, which is the confident expectation of divine blessing and eternal life with God (Catechism, no. 2090).

- Hope is not based on our own strength or ability to resist temptations, but on the mercy and goodness of God poured out upon us by the Holy Spirit (Catechism, no. 1817; cf. Rom. 5:5).

Questions for Reflection
or Group Discussion

1. How do I respond to the question, "Are you saved?"

2. How does the virtue of *hope* strike a balance between *presumption* ("my salvation is assured") and *despair* ("my sins are so bad God will never forgive me")?

3. Am I aware of my own sinful tendencies? Do I confidently ask for God's grace—especially through the sacraments—to persevere in the Christian life?

Chapter 10

SHOULD I OBEY?
Faithfully Responding to Lawful Authority

If someone in authority demands that I do something wrong, should I obey?

Obedience to lawful authority is an ordinary means of working out our salvation. As Saint Paul writes:

> Do you not know that if you yield yourselves to any one as obedient slaves, you are slaves of the one whom you obey, either of sin, which leads to death, or of obedience, which leads to righteousness? (Rom. 6:16).

Unfortunately today, many people are told to do things that they believe are wrong. Should they blindly obey? Or should they disobey and accept the negative consequences of such disobedience? This dilemma occurs frequently in the secular world and within the Church. For example, a business requires certain people to lie about profits and losses. Lying is a sin. Furthermore, if the lie results in obtaining money illegally, the act would contribute to theft. Not lying would shed bad light on the business and may result in the person losing his job. A bishop requires everyone in his diocese to stand during the consecration. Standing violates universal norms and does not signify reverence in the same way as kneeling. Not doing so leaves one open to criticism and even ridicule.

Before a decision is made to obey or disobey, each situation requires prudent discernment and prayerful consideration of certain principles. While these moral situations occur both in and out of the Church, this FAITH FACT will focus primarily on the issue as it relates to Church authorities. To better understand this issue and the role of authority, we strongly recommend reading the related FAITH FACTS noted in Appendix I.

Limits of Authority

"Let every person be subject to the governing authorities. For there is no authority except from God, and those that exist have been instituted by God" (Rom. 13:1; cf. Jn. 19:11). Those who hold authority share the authority of God, but in a limited way. While God's authority is absolute, man's is finite. God limits man's authority in two ways: by time and by office. The limit of time is easily understandable. There is a point in time when a man gains authority, and there is a point in time when he loses it. He naturally loses it at the time of death.

Limits of office are not as easy to understand. The term "office" refers to a stable position that gives the person in the position certain rights and obligations. These rights and obligations are the basis for authority attached to the office. Usually, both in secular society and within the Church, the authority held by an office is defined in writing. Those offices held within the Catholic Church are known as ecclesiastical offices, and canon law establishes their limits. These limits of authority depend to a great extent upon the nature of the particular ecclesiastical office and whether it is of divine or human origin (cf. canon 145 §2).

Furthermore, the jurisdiction of Church authority is territorial, personal, or both. Territorial jurisdiction refers to authority which can only be exercised within a particular geographical area, such as a parish or diocese. Anyone within this territory is subject to the lawful authority established there. Personal jurisdiction refers to authority that is exercised over particular people, no matter where they are. For example, religious are under obedience to their superiors no matter where they go. Their superiors exercise personal jurisdiction over them. Authority in the Church is usually limited by territorial jurisdiction, but there are many exceptions to this. For example, Bishop A has the authority to administer the Sacrament of Confirmation to anyone within his diocese, even to those who are merely visiting his diocese. However, Bishop B can expressly forbid his subjects from receiving this sacrament outside his diocese. Visitors from Bishop B's diocese could not, then, lawfully receive Confirmation from Bishop A within his territory (cf. canon 886 §1).

Common Good and Natural Rights

A basic obligation of all authority is service directed to the salvation of souls (cf. Jn. 13:14-15). This obligation is fulfilled when the common good is protected. By common good the Church means "the sum total of all those conditions of social life which enable individuals, families, and organizations to achieve complete and efficacious fulfillment" (GS 74; cf. Catechism, no. 1906). It concerns the good of everyone, and

> consist[s] of *three essential elements:* . . . *respect for the person* as such . . . the *social well-being* and *development* of the group itself . . . [and] *peace*, that is, the stability and security of a just order (Catechism, nos. 1906-09, original emphasis).

The common good is always oriented toward the progress of persons, and calls upon society to put persons ahead of things (cf. Catechism, no. 1912). This order is founded on truth, built up in justice, and animated by love.

The common good is never opposed to divine laws or the natural rights of an individual. Rather, divine laws establish both the common good and the natural rights that all people enjoy. Because divine laws cannot be in opposition, the common good and the natural rights of individuals complement and fulfill each other. Thus, decisions by those in authority should never violate natural rights of individuals, nor oppose the common good.

Divine Law or Discipline?

No one has authority to change or violate divine laws. All are bound by them, even the highest authorities in the Church. Any demand that requires a violation of divine law is a demand to sin, and no one is obligated to follow it.

Disciplines are man-made. Their purpose is to expound and apply divine laws in ways that fulfill the will of Christ and address the needs of our time. In this way, they further the common good and establish right order in the community. Because of the order they establish, they assist us in our salvation. Our Holy Father writes:

Christ the Lord, indeed, did not in the least wish to destroy
the very rich heritage of the law and the prophets which was
gradually formed from the history and experience of the people
of God in the Old Testament, but he brought it to completion
(cf. Mt. 5:17) such that in a new and higher way it became
part of the heritage of the New Testament. Therefore,
although in expounding the paschal mystery St. Paul teaches
that justification is not obtained by the works of the law but
by means of faith (cf. Rom. 3:28; Gal. 2:16), he does not thereby exclude the binding force of the Decalogue (cf. Rom. 13:28;
Gal. 5:13-25, 6:2), nor does he deny the importance of discipline in the Church of God (cf. 1 Cor. 5 and 6). Thus the
writings of the New Testament enable us to understand even
better the importance of discipline and make us see better
how it is more closely connected with the saving character of
the evangelical message itself. . . . [Rather than substituting
for faith, grace, and charisms,] its purpose is rather to create
such an order in the ecclesial society that, while assigning the
primacy to love, grace and charisms, it at the same time ren-
ders their organic development easier in the life of both the
ecclesial society and the individual persons who belong to it.[1]

Some disciplines are more important than others. Some
arise from customs, others from written laws. Violations of
some disciplines are more serious than violations of others.
Depending on their nature and importance, some disciplines
can be dispensed or changed by a bishop or someone approved
by him, while others require an act from the Holy See.

In most instances, pastors only have the authority to enforce,
not make or change, disciplines. For example, it is not lawful for
a Catholic to marry a baptized non-Catholic without proper
permission. Such permission is usually given by diocesan offi-
cials through the local pastor when he prepares the couple for
marriage. If the permission is not given, and the priest witnesses
the marriage, the marriage is valid but unlawful. However,

---

[1] Pope John Paul II, Apostolic Constitution Promulgating the 1983 Code of Canon
Law *Sacrae Disciplinae Leges,* as found in *Code of Canon Law, Latin-English Edition*
(Washington: Canon Law Society of America, 1983), xiii-xiv.

consecration of a bishop requires the permission of the Holy See or all involved are excommunicated (cf. canon 1382). While permission is necessary in both cases, the violation of the first discipline is less serious than a violation of the second.

Also, certain liturgical norms are under the authority of the local bishop or conference of bishops, while others cannot be modified without the approval of Rome. For example, the use of extraordinary ministers and female altar servers are issues the local bishop can address. Changing one of the authorized Eucharistic Prayers requires an act of the Holy See.

If a violation of divine law is demanded, no one is obliged to obey. However, when changes in culture and the needs of the common good occur, changes in a related discipline should also occur in order to promote the common good and protect right order. These changes in discipline cannot occur without the approval of lawful authority. If a violation of Church discipline is demanded, one should take care not to offend lawful authority or the common good by refusing to obey. Rather, one should carefully consider the subject matter, its nature and importance, and whether the one making the demand has the authority to make the demand. Importantly, one should also consider the common good, and whether refusal to obey will promote right order or chaos.

Sin and Scandal

When discerning whether to obey, one must consider the consequences of each alternative. We have a God-given obligation to avoid sin but, if the action demanded is not of itself sinful, can we disobey without offending the one in authority or without scandal? This is an important question. When Church authorities demand obedience to an action that violates Church law, the act itself usually is not sinful. However, our disobedience in such a situation could cause scandal, which itself is a sin (cf. Catechism, no. 2284).

For example, in the Western Church, standing during the consecration is not prescribed by the liturgical books. In the Eastern Churches, there is a long-standing tradition that the faithful never kneel during the Easter Season. They remain standing, even through the consecration. This demonstrates that standing during the consecration is not in itself sinful. What could be sinful is the interior disposition of the heart. If one reverences Christ in his heart, but cannot kneel, Christ is reverenced. If one kneels, but does not reverence Christ in his heart, Christ is not reverenced. If a priest demands that the congregation stand during the consecration—and none of the recognized exceptions to the general rule applies—this demand violates liturgical law. The priest is wrong to do this. However, his demand does not change the disposition of the congregation. It changes only a posture. Before refusing to obey, one should consider the consequences and avoid sin in all its forms, particularly sins associated with detraction (cf. Catechism, no. 2479) and scandal.

Right to Question Authority

Those in authority are not without weaknesses. They make mistakes. They sin. Because of these facts, the Catholic Church recognizes and protects the right to question lawful authority. The Church also recognizes the need to protect the common good and avoid scandal when questioning lawful authority. Because of the rights and obligations attached to ecclesiastical offices and the need to protect right order, the Church always presumes good faith on the part of lawful authority, and she always presumes their actions are in accord with law. She expects the faithful to make these same presumptions. To protect the common good, the Church has established various procedures to be used when questioning the actions of those in authority. As explained in the Code of Canon Law:

> **Canon 212 §1:** The Christian faithful, conscious of their own responsibility, are bound by Christian obedience to follow what the sacred pastors, as representatives of Christ, declare as teachers of the faith or determine as leaders of the Church.

> **§3:** In accord with the knowledge, competence and preeminence which they possess, they have the right and even at times a duty to manifest to the sacred pastors their opinion on matters which pertain to the good of the Church, and they have a right to make their opinion known to the other

Christian faithful, with due regard for the integrity of faith and morals and reverence toward their pastors, and with consideration for the common good and the dignity of persons.

Canon 221 §1: The Christian faithful can legitimately vindicate and defend the rights which they enjoy in the Church before a competent ecclesiastical forum in accord with the norm of law.

In short, while we have a right to question authority, we have an obligation to do so only according to the means provided by the Church (see Appendix II). These means safeguard the common good against scandal and protect the reputations of everyone involved. If we question lawful authority according to the means provided by the Church, we remain obedient to the Church. If we use unlawful means that cause scandal and destroy reputations, we become guilty of disobedience and detraction, even if the one in authority is wrong.

Holy Docility

CUF founder H. Lyman Stebbins, in correspondence dated December 26, 1977, aptly summed up the proper disposition of the laity toward authority:

The history of the Holy Church almost begins with the sinful denial by the first pope, and by the desertion of the other apostles: and that history has continued through time with a perfectly open record of the failings of popes and bishops. The historical record is there. The practical question for you and me is: What, then, are we to make of the words of Christ: "They that hear you hear Me?" of the words: "If he will not hear the Church, let him be to thee as the publican and heathen." Of the words of councils and popes throughout the ages (especially the Council of Trent, Vatican I, and Vatican II) which teach that we must be docile to our bishops as bishops. If, on a Monday, my bishop commands me to commit a sin, I must disobey him; but he remains my bishop; and if, the very next day, in his office as bishop, he commands me to receive Holy Communion standing, I must obey him.

Questions for Reflection
or Group Discussion

1. What is my attitude toward authority in the Church? What is my disposition toward the Holy Father? My bishop? My pastor?

2. How do misuses of authority affect my attitude toward authority figures? How do I respect authority in such circumstances without sinning or causing scandal?

3. What can I do to encourage those in authority in the Church? How can I foster unity within the Church when I'm asked to do something that seems wrong?

4. How do I determine whether to obey a particular directive from my bishop or pastor? What principles apply? What presumptions am I obliged to make? Why would I ever choose to disobey?

Chapter 11

MARRIAGE IN GOD'S PLAN
Discovering the Power of Marital Love

What is the role of marriage in the plan of God?

Christ restored marriage to its original integrity and elevated it to the dignity of a sacrament. Marriage reflects the communion of love that the Godhead shares in Himself and is a means through which God restores man to the communion for which he was created.

In order to grasp the full meaning and power of marriage, we must understand why man was created. The first paragraph of the Catechism teaches that God created man freely, out of sheer goodness, so that all might share eternal life with Him (cf. Eph. 1:3-10; 2 Pet. 1:4).

In his apostolic exhortation *Familiaris Consortio*, Pope John Paul II further explains:

> God created man in His own image and likeness: calling him to existence *through love*, He called him at the same time *for love*. God is love and in Himself He lives a mystery of personal loving communion. Creating the human race in His own image and continually keeping it in being, God inscribed in the humanity of man and woman the vocation, and thus the capacity and responsibility, of love and communion. Love is therefore the fundamental and innate vocation of every human being (no. 11, original emphasis, footnotes omitted).

God Created Man for Love

Man's deepest vocation as a person is to love God. This also entails loving one's neighbor, who is created in the image and likeness of God. Christ called loving God and neighbor the greatest of all the commandments (cf. Mk. 12:29-31), and Saint Paul taught that the fulfilling of the law is to love (cf. Rom. 13:8-10).

God Himself "lives a mystery of personal loving communion." God made man in His image and likeness to share in that loving communion, not out of His own need, but purely as an act of goodness. Marital love is a striking image of the kind of love that God lives in Himself and that which we were created to share with Him. This was so from the beginning.

The concept of marriage is central to all of Scripture. It begins with the creation of man (Gen. 1-3) and ends with a vision of the wedding feast of the Lamb (Rev. 21-22; cf. Catechism, no. 1602). God's covenant with His people Israel is revealed in marital imagery. We find this throughout the Old Testament, particularly in the books of the Prophets, the Song of Solomon, and the story of Ruth and Boaz.

In the New Testament, marriage expresses the intimate relationship between Christ and the Church (Eph. 5:22; Rev. 21:2, 9). In His parables, Jesus often employs the image of marriage (e.g., Mt. 22:1-14; 25:1-13). Further, Holy Mother Church has always attached great significance to the fact that Jesus' first miracle was at the wedding in Cana.

Because it expresses the love of God for His people, marriage serves God's ultimate purpose and plan for humanity. It served that purpose prior to the severing of that unity by sin. As a sacrament, in Christ, it serves to restore that unity.

At the Service of Communion

The Catechism describes marriage as a sacrament at the service of communion (nos. 1534-35). This means that it is directed toward the salvation of others. Other sacraments contribute in various ways to the salvation of the recipient. Those at the service of communion, when one receives them, are given to contribute to the salvation of another.

Sacramental marriage consecrates spouses to a special dignity. They are called to fulfill certain duties (ibid., no. 1535). What are these duties? How is it that marriage actually ministers God's grace to individuals on their path to eternal life? The meaning of marriage from the beginning was one of love and communion, reflecting the very image of God. For this reason, after the scourge of sin, Christ redeemed marital love to effect the restoration of that communion of love for which man was first created (cf. Catechism, no. 1615). Therefore, the single most important duty or task of married love is to be at the service of communion. This clearly means that spouses bear a certain responsibility for each other's salvation, and together for that of their children. From this fundamental obligation all other duties and responsibilities of marriage flow.

To understand how to restore communion with God, we must first understand communion itself. There are several aspects to consider.

Communion: The Personal Touch

Communion is possible only between persons. A person is not a mere instance of a species, let alone an interchangeable commodity. Rather, each person is unique and unrepeatable; he is himself and not another. A person is never merely a part of a larger whole, but an individual "I."[1]

Love is the only adequate response to persons. This is what Pope John Paul II calls the "personalistic norm."[2] A person can never be used as a means to an end, but must be viewed as an end in himself. In marriage, a spouse is loved for his or her own sake. Marital love, then, is a value-response[3] to the intrinsic beauty and worth of the beloved. Love becomes the cause of a radically new and different kind of communion.

Communion: Sexuality

One should not mistakenly think that the only difference between spousal love and other relationships is sex. The

---

[1] For a fuller explanation and development of these ideas, see John F. Crosby, *The Selfhood of the Human Person* (Washington: Catholic University of America Press, 1996); Karol Wojtyla, "The Subjectivity and Irreducible in Man," *Person and Community: Selected Essays* (Washington: Catholic University of America Press, 1993), trans. by Theresa Sandok.

[2] Karol Wojtyla, *Love and Responsibility* (San Francisco: Ignatius Press, 1993), 40-44.

[3] Dietrich von Hildebrand, *Ethics* (Chicago: Franciscan Herald Press, 1972), ch. 17.

difference is that the nature of marriage requires total self-donation and self-giving of one person to another that is completely indissoluble. Sexual union is intrinsically a part of this and, for this reason, is proper only to marriage.

Sexuality, then, is much more than a biological function or a mere urge or physical instinct within marital love. Spousal love is between persons and human persons have bodies. Sexual union is not merely the satisfaction of a bodily instinct, but part of the mutual self-giving of the spouses. In sexual union, spouses are not merely giving their bodies to each other as if the self could be momentarily suspended, but they are giving their very selves to one another with their bodies. This is why, outside of the indissoluble covenant of marriage, sex is always a lie and is always the use of another person for self-satisfaction. In such acts, the couple does not act like persons in the image and likeness of God, but like mere animals.

Communion: Children

The call to be fruitful and multiply (Gen. 1:28) is part of spousal love. The procreation and education of children is the primary end of marriage, and it cannot be understood as such outside the context of the meaning of marriage, which is love. Did God command procreation merely to populate the earth, using man and woman as a means to that end? No. To be fruitful and multiply follows the unique union of man and woman in the image of God in love.

The true beauty of procreation lies in the fact that it flows from marital love. As sexual union is much more than a mere biological function, so is procreation. It is so intensely beautiful and powerful that from this loving act a new, unique person comes into being with all the characteristics of a person mentioned above. The spouses are then called to train their children in the school of love, so that each may discover his or her vocation as a child of God. Here we can clearly see marriage as a sacrament at the service of communion, as spouses fulfill their mission to raise godly children and truly function as a "domestic Church" (cf. Catechism, nos. 1656, 2221-26).

It is sad when a person ignores the value of the other and uses the other for sexual satisfaction alone—even within marriage. When this happens, the value of the child is not reduced, because such value is intrinsic to the child.[4] However, the spouses deprive one another of the full power of their sexual union and may not appreciate the child's incalculable worth. The connection between sex and procreation is far more profound than the mere biology of human reproduction.

This is why every contraceptive act is an offense against spousal love. Contraception not only frustrates procreation, but it strikes at the very heart of procreation, which is spousal love. It is irredeemably depersonalizing. Natural Family Planning, in contrast, when used as intended by the Church, fosters respect for the person in marriage. On the one hand, we are not to frustrate the possibility of conception in the marital act. On the other hand, our bodies are not mere machines to produce offspring indiscriminately. If this were so, the sexual union of a couple who could not conceive would possess less value than those who procreate. This is absurd. The value lies in the love and communion of spouses, while children are the "supreme gift" that God in His loving providence may bestow on this union (cf. GS 50).

The Sanctifying Power of Marital Love

Through their mutual, self-giving love, spouses actually participate in each other's sanctification. They become a channel through which Christ confers grace to live the Christian life. Saint Paul writes, "Husbands, love your wives, as Christ loved the church and gave himself up for her, that he might sanctify her, having cleansed her by the washing of water with the word" (Eph. 5:25-26). This speaks of total self-giving, as Christ gave Himself for us. The submission of wives to husbands in the same passage is not an issue of equality or a designation of

---

[4] The value of a child is not measured by the degree of love in the sexual act. But since a human person of inestimable worth is created by this act, the beauty and sacredness of the act must be respected.

value, but a response to that love.[5] As the Bride of Christ, the Church—and thus all her members—are called to love Christ without holding anything back.

The sanctifying power of marital love is so great that the Apostle Paul says even an unbelieving spouse is sanctified by the believing one, and thus the children are also holy (1 Cor. 7:14). When couples do not love each other in total self-donation, they fail to fulfill completely the high calling of marriage. Sin is the cause of the struggle, yet we must strive to love as Jesus loves. We must take advantage of every means possible to grow in holiness and perfect ourselves, especially through the sacraments.

God calls each family to foster a "civilization of love." It is first in the Christian family that new persons are introduced into the world. Through this family, the "first herald" of the Gospel (LG 11), children are introduced into God's wider family, the Church. The family, then, is the school of social life and a deeper humanity. To understand these points, every Christian should read *Familiaris Consortio* as well as the rich teaching on marriage in the Catechism.

Total Gift of Self

Man's communion with God is the reason for which he was created. The Sacrament of Matrimony serves this purpose in its own unique way with the other sacraments of the Church. It must be kept in mind that Christ restored marriage to its original integrity and elevated it to the dignity of a sacrament (cf. Mt. 19:3-9; Catechism, nos. 1614-17, 1660). If we are to grasp the full impact of marriage as a sacrament, it must first be understood what it is in itself—a deep and intimate communion of persons.

> Like each of the seven sacraments, so also marriage is a real symbol of the event of salvation, but in its own way. "The

---

[5] In Ephesians 5:21, Saint Paul makes clear that there is a mutual submission between the spouses. Verse 22 explains how each must submit to the other. This is clearly explained by Pope John Paul II in his Apostolic Letter On the Dignity and Vocation of Women *Mulieris Dignitatem* (1988), especially no. 29.

spouses participate in it as spouses, together, as a couple, so that the first and immediate effect of marriage (*res et sacramentum*) is not supernatural grace itself, but the Christian conjugal bond, a typically Christian communion of two persons because it represents the mystery of Christ's incarnation and the mystery of His covenant. The content of participation in Christ's life is also specific: Conjugal love involves a totality, in which all the elements of the person enter—appeal of the body and instinct, power of feeling and affectivity, aspiration of the spirit and of will. It aims at a deeply personal unity, the unity that, beyond union in one flesh, leads to forming one heart and soul; it demands indissolubility and faithfulness in definitive mutual giving; and it is open to fertility (cf. HV 9). In a word it is a question of the normal characteristics of all natural conjugal love, but with a new significance which not only purifies and strengthens them, but raises them to the extent of making them the expression of specifically Christian values" (FC 13).[6]

Questions for Reflection or Group Discussion

1. Marriage is a Christian vocation. What does this mean to me? What is the mission of Christian spouses?

2. (For married persons) Do I give totally of myself to my spouse? Do I understand sexual intercourse as a total gift of myself, and not merely as a biological act? Am I open to the gift of children and the mission of parenthood? How do I draw upon the grace of the Sacrament of Marriage?

3. What couples have best modeled for me the ideal of Christian marriage? What is it about these marriages that most impresses me?

---

[6] This text quotes from Pope John Paul II's "Address to the Delegates of the Centre de Liaison des Équipes de Recherche" (November 3, 1979).

Chapter 12

CHOOSE LIFE, THAT YOU AND YOUR CHILDREN MAY LIVE
The Truth About Birth Control

Is artificial birth control or contraception ever permitted?

Under no circumstances is the use of contraception morally permissible. This is the clear and infallible teaching of the Catholic Church and, because it flows from the natural law as given to us by God, the Creator of all people, it is binding on all men and women (HV 18; Catechism, no. 2036).[1]

Gospel of Life

The Roman Catholic Church's teaching that contraception is always and everywhere wrong is very controversial today. Like the disciples who walked away from Jesus, many say, "This is a hard saying; who can listen to it?" (Jn. 6:60). Like Christ Himself, it is a "sign of contradiction" (Lk. 2:34), a "stumbling block" (1 Pet. 2:8) in a society that has largely rejected sexual morality in favor of what Pope John Paul II calls a "culture of death."

---

[1] The term "contraception" does not apply to the use of Natural Family Planning (see pp. 112-113), nor to the use of interventions intended for a purpose other than the exclusion of children during sexual intercourse between a consenting man and woman. For example, certain medical conditions require the use of steroid treatments to regulate a woman's cycles. As a medical treatment to aid in the health of a woman, this is not wrong. However, this treatment may have the same effects as the pill. Further, such treatment may not entirely suppress ovulation, and thus act as an abortifacient if conception occurs. If this is the case, a serious reason must exist for a woman to use such treatment if she is having marital relations while taking the treatment. Provided that a sufficiently grave reason exists, and she takes precautions to avoid intercourse during potentially fertile periods, it is morally acceptable to receive such treatments.

The Church, the "pillar and bulwark of the truth" (1 Tim. 3:15), will never succumb to the thinking of the world (cf. Rom. 12:2) and to the snares of the evil one, who is the "father of lies" and a "murderer from the beginning" (Jn. 8:44). Rather, the Church is a mother who never forgets her children (cf. Is. 49:15). The Gospel of Life, which reveals God's loving plan for every human person, is a call to each of us to reform our lives—including our sexuality—in conformity with the Gospel. Even more, it is a call to an ever-deepening relationship with God the Father, the Author of all life, and Jesus Christ whom He sent (cf. Jn. 17:3).

Contraception frustrates the purpose of the marital act as the proper expression of love between husband and wife, and is opposed to the virtue of chastity in marriage (EV 13; cf. Catechism, no. 2349). Legitimate reasons on the part of spouses to avoid a new birth do not justify recourse to morally unacceptable ("intrinsically evil") means, such as contraception or direct sterilization (Catechism, nos. 2370, 2399; cf. EV 97).

There are many objections to the Church's teaching on contraception. Some believe it is inconvenient and impractical, if not outright impossible. Others believe it is foolish and irresponsible in a world that is apparently overpopulated. Still others consider contraception and all aspects of their personal lives as private choices to be made according to their individual determination of what's best for them. Some will even argue that if the Catholic Church were truly opposed to abortion, it would allow for contraception. They reason that if couples could contracept, they wouldn't need to abort.

Each of these notions is false and needs to be refuted.

Objection #1:
Ban on Contraception Is Impractical

Self-control is difficult, but with God's grace it is not impossible. Those who maintain that couples cannot remain chaste and open to life bear witness to the fact that sin holds us in slavery and impairs our ability to freely choose the good. Yet Christ has come to liberate us from the slavery of sin and death (cf. Rom. 6:17-23), and history is filled with examples of chaste and heroically generous people.

Hedonism—the pursuit of self-gratification—is the opposite of true love, because true love is not selfish or self-seeking (cf. 1 Cor. 13:4-7), but involves a total gift of self to others. Christ manifested His love for us by giving Himself up for us on the Cross. Spouses are called to imitate this love through their mutual self-gift.

The secular entertainment and advertising media promotes hedonism, as do attitudes and, sadly, sex education programs that assume that self-control is impossible. Because they assume self-control is impossible, they promote contraception as a means of ensuring "safe sex." This is tantamount to treating ourselves and our children as animals, not human persons who have been created in God's image, redeemed by Christ's blood, and reborn as "new creations" (2 Cor. 5:17) through the power of the Holy Spirit.

Hedonism is frequently the engine behind the desire to drive a wedge between the unitive (love-giving) and procreative (life-giving) aspects of the sexual act. Hedonism wants the pleasure of sexual intercourse without the responsibility. However, sexual intercourse that is deliberately closed to new life is inherently selfish, not "unitive." The sexual act, which was made by God to be the ultimate expression of marital love, becomes tragically cheapened by contraception into a means for using others to satisfy one's own desires. All people want to be loved; nobody really wants to be used.

Objection #2:
The Myth of Overpopulation

The myth of overpopulation is many-faceted.

Actually, the world is comparatively empty. There are approximately 52.5 million square miles of land in the world, not including Antarctica. In 1997, the world's population was 5.9 billion. By allowing 3.5 square feet per person, all the people in the world could be brought together in the city of Jacksonville, Florida. While everyone would admittedly be cramped in Jacksonville, it would be possible to allot each individual person 1,000 square feet (4,000 square feet of living space for a family of four) and still fit the entire world's population in the states of Nebraska, Kansas, and South

Dakota, leaving the rest of the United States, plus Canada, Mexico, Central and South America, Europe, Africa, Asia, and the Australian South Pacific areas completely uninhabited by man.[2]

Pope John Paul II exposes the lie of overpopulation for what it really is: a "conspiracy against life."

> The Pharaoh of old, haunted by the presence and increase of the children of Israel, submitted them to every kind of oppression and ordered that every male child born of the Hebrew women was to be killed (cf. Ex. 1:7-22). Today not a few of the powerful of the earth act in the same way (EV 16).

There are, however, serious problems concerning the distribution of the earth's goods. But this poor distribution is the result of sin, not overpopulation. Many of the world's calamities and starvation problems are caused by political corruption within third world countries and a lack of generosity on the part of those individuals and nations with greater abundance. With modern agricultural equipment, adequate food storage facilities, and technology to ensure clean drinking water, third world countries like India could make great strides in becoming self-sufficient. Developed countries like the United States could help provide these improvements.

Unfortunately, instead of really investing in development and self-sufficiency, superpowers like the United States have coercively tied financial aid to the acceptance of condoms and abortifacient (abortion-inducing) contraceptives as a means to control these countries. Genuine development, not a surplus of contraceptives, is what these countries truly need. As the Church affirms, people are a country's greatest resource (see also EV 16).

So corrupt governmental policies—not overpopulation—cause the majority of problems cited as evidence for overpopulation.

---

[2] Rick and Jan Hess, A *Full Quiver* (Brentwood, TN: Wolgemuth & Hyatt, Publishers, Inc., 1989), 72-77.

Objection #3:
It's a Personal Decision

All truly human actions are personal decisions, and involve personal freedom. However, having the freedom to choose does not make all choices good. When we freely make bad choices, choices that injure our relationships with God and others, we sin.

And so the conscience, our "inner sanctuary," must be submissive to the truth. That is truly the key to happiness in this life and the next. Sadly, many people today have exchanged a conscience formed by the light of Christ and His Church for a conscience that is independent from objective morality. That's why the Catechism (no. 1792) cites a "mistaken notion of autonomy of conscience" as a "source of errors of judgment in moral conduct."[3]

The notion that each person can choose—at least to a certain extent—what the guiding principles of morality are is known as *moral relativism*, a concept the U.S. Supreme Court tragically endorsed in a 1992 decision regarding abortion: "At the heart of liberty is the right to define one's own concept of existence, of meaning, of the universe, and of the mystery of human life."[4] Without necessarily setting out to do so, those who embrace moral relativism usurp God's role as author and judge of His creation. Not surprisingly, Cardinal Joseph Ratzinger, head of the Vatican Congregation for the Doctrine of the Faith, frequently refers to such relativism (often manifested as "cafeteria Catholicism") as the central problem for the faith at the present time.

Objection #4:
Contraception Will Reduce Abortion

This claim is patently false. The introduction of contraception dramatically increases abortion as well as the breakdown of families, divorce, and sexual relationships outside of marriage. In these cases, the illusory claim of "safe sex" leads to the inevitable failure of contraceptive devices.

---

[3] See generally chapter 8, "Going God's Way."
[4] *Planned Parenthood v. Casey*, 120 L.Ed. 2d 674, 698 (1992).

As Father Paul Marx, O.S.B., a veteran pro-life leader, has noted, the legalization of abortion has followed in every country whose government and populace have embraced and promoted contraception. In the United States, the constitutional "right to privacy" declared by the U.S. Supreme Court to legitimize interstate trade of contraceptives (*Griswold v. Connecticut*, 1965) eventually served as the basis for making abortion on demand the law of the land (*Roe v. Wade*, 1973).

Couples not wanting to conceive will frequently resort to abortion as a final measure of contraception. Almost two decades following *Roe v. Wade*, Supreme Court Justice Anthony Kennedy upheld the "right" to abortion partly because reproductive choices are now made based on the judicially created expectation that abortion would be available in the event contraception should fail.[5]

Pope John Paul II has also recognized the connection between abortion and contraception, noting that both

> are rooted in a hedonistic mentality unwilling to accept responsibility in matters of sexuality, and they imply a self-centered concept of freedom, which regards procreation as an obstacle to personal fulfillment. The life which could result from a sexual encounter thus becomes an enemy to be avoided at all costs, and abortion becomes the only possible decisive response to failed contraception (EV 13).

God's Plan for Marital Love

The Catholic vision of marital love and, indeed, the Judeo-Christian tradition bearing witness to thousands of years of divine Revelation, present a completely different perspective. Within the Judeo-Christian understanding, sexual relations are reserved for marriage. The Scriptures are clear that fornication (sexual relations before marriage) and adultery (sexual relations with someone other than one's spouse) are absolutely forbidden and condemned as a serious breach of God's will. Why is this

---

[5] *Ibid.*

the case? From the very beginning, Almighty God created man within the family. In Genesis, God said: "Let us make man in our image, after our likeness. . . . So God created man in his own image, in the image of God he created him; male and female he created them" (Gen. 1:26-27).

God created the first man and the first woman within the framework of a marital relationship, a family. They were to imitate God in whose image and likeness they were created. In Jesus Christ, we realize the fullness of God's plan for us. At the heart of the Christian Revelation is the mystery of the Trinity. It is the mystery of God in Himself. It is therefore the source of all other mysteries of faith, the light that enlightens them. It is the most fundamental and essential in the "hierarchy of the truths of faith" (Catechism, no. 234).

From all of eternity, God the Father, who is all good, all holy, and all true, has given of Himself completely and totally. This gift is so perfect that it is the eternal Son, who is God from God, Light from Light, True God from True God (Nicene Creed). Because the Son is equally God and the perfect reflection of the Father, who is all good, all true, and all holy, He imitates the Father and in turn gives of Himself completely and totally. This mutual self-gift of the Father and the Son is the Holy Spirit, the Third Person of the Trinity and the bond of unity in love within the Godhead.

We have been created to imitate, with God's help, the life of the Holy Trinity. In marriage, husband and wife are called to give themselves completely, holding nothing back, in imitation of the Trinity, whose gift of self is perfect. At the heart of the marriage is the marital act. And as husband and wife give themselves completely and totally to one another, they imitate God and, in so doing, may be blessed with a child. To hold back, to say no, to turn away from this gift of self and from an openness to the action of God, is a sin against God, one's spouse, and the deepest, most intimate part of oneself. The act of contraception attacks our ability to image God, to behave in His likeness. With God's grace, the couple is invited to welcome life and, when children are given, to continue freely giving to them throughout their lives, raising them up in an atmosphere of heroic generosity and love, pouring out goodness and truth, and caring for one another. In this type of love, as with God, there is no room for selfishness.

This teaching is challenging and at times even frightening, but it is the truth. Even without divine Revelation, the natural law bears witness in the heart of every man and woman that the act of contraception, including taking the pill or making use of a device to oppose the conception of a child in the midst of the marital act (cf. Catechism, no. 2370), runs contrary to marital love. In fact, contraception makes a lie of the total, self-giving love our sexuality was intended to express.

Natural Family Planning

On the other hand, the Church recognizes the natural right of parents to determine the number and spacing of births for just reasons. These reasons can take into account psychological and physical conditions of the father or mother and the obligations the parents have toward themselves, other children, extended family, and society in general. However, limiting and spacing births can be done without offending moral principles only if Natural Family Planning is used.[6] As Pope Paul VI taught:

> The Church is coherent with herself when she maintains that recourse to the infertile periods is licit, while at the same time condemning, as being always illicit, the use of means which directly prevent conception, even if such use is inspired by reasons which may appear honest and serious. In reality, there are essential differences between the two cases. In the former case the married couple make legitimate use of a natural disposition; in the latter they impede the development of natural processes. It is true that, in either case, the married couple mutually agree in the positive will of avoiding children for plausible reasons, seeking the certainty that offspring will not arrive. But it is also true that only in the former case are they able to renounce the use of marriage in the fertile periods when, for just motives, procreation is not desirable, while

---

[6] Cf. HV 16; Holy See, *Charter of Rights of the Family* (October 22, 1983), art. 3; Catechism, no. 2370.

making use of it during infertile periods to manifest their affection and to safeguard their mutual fidelity. By so doing, they give proof of a truly and integrally honest love (HV 16).

The consequences of openness to life are expensive. Children require a great deal of care, energy, time, and resources. The demands that they place upon us may seem at times overwhelming. However, we are not free to deny the truth that they are a supreme gift from God (GS 50) and that we should willingly accept them. If we suppress this truth, we will inevitably turn our backs on God (cf. Rom. 1:18-25).

Prophetic Voice of the Church

Judeo-Christian tradition has consistently and unswervingly opposed contraception, dating back to the contraceptive act of Onan in Genesis 38:9. Some argue that God struck down Onan not because he contracepted, but because of his refusal to provide children to his brother's widow. However, such "levirate" laws were not enacted until long after the events of Genesis 38 and, in any event, Deuteronomy 25:5-10 refutes this interpretation, because the refusal "to perpetuate his brother's name" only resulted in a man's public humiliation, not his death.

Interestingly, Martin Luther, the founder of Protestantism, condemned the act of contraception in stern words:

This is a most disgraceful sin. It is far more atrocious than incest and adultery. We call it unchastity, yes, a Sodomitic sin. For Onan goes into her; that is, he lies with and copulates, and when it comes to the point of insemination, spills the semen, lest the woman conceive. Surely at such a time the order of nature established by God in procreation should be followed. . . . He committed an evil deed. Therefore God punished him.[7]

---

[7] Martin Luther, "Commentary on Genesis 38:8-10," as quoted in Charles Provan, *The Bible and Birth Control* (Monongahela, PA: Zimmer Printing, 1989), 80-81.

Christianity was of one accord in the condemnation of contraception until 1930, when the Church of England repudiated
Christian tradition and allowed for contraception. By 1950 and
the advent of the birth control pill, many other groups began
to defect as well, so that at this time the Roman Catholic
Church is an almost solitary voice, bearing witness to the timeless truth manifested in the Psalms:

> Lo, sons are a heritage from the Lord, the fruit of the womb a
> reward. Like arrows in the hand of a warrior are the sons of
> one's youth. Happy is the man who has his quiver full of them!
> (Ps. 127:3-5; cf. Ps. 128).

Perhaps nowhere else are the lies of the contraceptive men-
tality more striking than in the cover-up of the truth about the
abortifacient effects of many "contraceptive devices." Many
commonly used birth control devices allow conception, but kill
the child shortly thereafter. These include, but are not limited
to, the IUD (the intrauterine device) and the birth control pill.
In their 1994 publication *Birth Control and Christian
Discipleship*, the Couple to Couple League reports that
2,950,000 early abortions are caused by the IUD each year in
the United States. Between 2 million and 4 million early abortions are caused by the implantation-resisting effects of the pill
in the United States.[8]

As noted, these statistics refer only to the United States.
Throughout the world, an estimated 250 million abortions are
caused by the IUD and pill each year. This almost equals the
population of the United States, and exceeds the population of
most countries in the world today.

At the time of Adam and Eve's original sin, God warned that
the devil would strike at the offspring of the "woman" (Gen.
3:15). He also promised that the "woman" and her offspring
would prevail (cf. Mt. 1:23-23; Lk. 1:26-35; Rev. 12:1-6). The

---

[8] John F. Kippley, *Birth Control and Christian Discipleship* (Cincinnati: Couple to
Couple League, 1994), 14.

only answer to the dishonesty and tragedy of birth control is Jesus, who is the way, the truth, and the life (Jn. 14:6). To eradicate this serious evil in our world today, we only have to take seriously our vocation as Christians and choose life, that we and our children may live (Deut. 30:19).

_____*SideBar*___

The Arithmetic of Abortifacient Birth Control

Unobstructed intercourse at the fertile time does not always result in pregnancy. However, the probability of conception occurring for a couple not using anticonception devices (condom, diaphragm, and spermicides) is at least 25% in any given cycle among normally fertile couples of average sexual activity, and it ranges up to 68% for couples who have relations every day during the fertile time. The lower figure (25%) will be used in describing the magnitude of early abortions with the IUD and the Pill; it is conservative relative to the coital patterns stated by Kinsey for American couples where wives are under 40. Thus, a pregnancy rate of .25 in each cycle among one million women using IUDs every cycle would result in 250,000 conceptions per month. An average of 12 menstrual-fertility cycles per year would yield 3,000,000 IUD-caused early abortions. However, since the IUD has about a 5% surprise pregnancy rate, among 1,000,000 IUD users in the U.S.A., there would be approximately 50,000 recognized pregnancies each year, many to be killed later by surgical abortion. Subtracting these 50,000 from the directly IUD caused abortions yields an estimated 2,950,000 early abortions each year caused by the IUD. Multiply that by 84 for the estimate of the world total— 247,800,000 early abortions each year.

Estimates about the number of abortions caused by the Pill are more difficult because of the triple-threat action of the Pill. The older high dosage pills had "breakthrough ovulation" rates of between 2% and 10%; given the lower dosage in today's Pills and the numbers of women using the mini-pill which apparently has almost no suppression of ovulation, the 10% figure does not seem unreasonable to use, but we can calculate it both ways. Among the 13.8 million American women using the Pill, the 10% rate would yield 1,380,000 ovulatory cycles each month. Applying the 25% overall conception rate would yield 345,000 conceptions each month or 4,140,000 new lives each year, almost all of which would be aborted by the implantation-resisting effects of the Pill.

A 4.7% rate of breakthrough ovulation was observed and reported in 1984. Applying that rate to the 13.8 million American women on the Pill would yield 648,600 ovulations and an estimated 162,150 new lives conceived each cycle, or 1,945,800 each year, almost all of whom would be denied implantation and thus aborted.

Even if you want to use the low 2% breakthrough ovulation rate, a figure I think is too low considering the lower dosages and the mini-pill today, you will end up with over 800,000 early abortions per year from the Pill alone, about half as many as from surgical abortion. And again, such figures are only for the United States and would need to be multiplied by 4.3 times for the rest of the world.

—John F. Kippley
Birth Control and Christian Discipleship, 14

Questions for Reflection
or Group Discussion

1. Do I understand that contraception and abortion are "fruits of the same tree" (EV 13)? How are they related? How are they distinct? How would I counter the objection that the widespread availability of contraception is the most effective remedy against abortion?

2. How does contraception change the marital act? Why shouldn't consenting adults be able to do what they want in the privacy of their bedroom?

3. Some spouses have legitimate reasons to forego having children for a period of time. For them, the Church warmly recommends Natural Family Planning (NFP). Read Catechism, nos. 2368-70. How is NFP different from contraception? Isn't it just a fancy name for Catholic birth control?

4. The Church's teaching on contraception is a "hard saying" for many, including many Catholics who really want to obey Church teaching. How can I, through word, example, and practical assistance, help others to embrace this teaching joyfully?

Chapter 13

MALE AND FEMALE HE CREATED THEM
The Church and "Same-Sex Marriages"

Why does the Church oppose government-sanctioned homosexual "marriages"?

Two men cannot legitimately marry each other, nor can two women, no matter what any earthly judicial or legislative body may say. Marriage is by nature defined by the conjugal act between one man and one woman, a monogamous or exclusive union in which the two become one in a lifelong partnership (cf. Gen. 2:24; Mt. 19:4-6).

This truth is understandable not only through divine Revelation, but also through natural reason. For by nature, man and woman are made for each other. They complement each other both physically and socially. In contrast, homosexual relationships are unnatural and do not contribute to the growth of society. In fidelity to the teachings of Christ, the Catholic Church opposes homosexual activity and state approval of homosexual relationships.

The Catholic Church teaches that Christ elevated marriage to the level of a sacrament. A husband and his wife are called to imitate and participate in the nuptial union of Christ and His bride, the Church (cf. Eph. 5:21-33), in a communion of life and love that is open to the gift of children (cf. Catechism, no. 1652).

God created man in His image and likeness. He created them male and female, so that through marriage they might reflect the communal love of the Holy Trinity (cf. Gen. 1:26-28). From all eternity, the Father pours His entire being into His Son, and the Son into the Father. The eternal bond of love between Father and Son is the Holy Spirit, the Third Person of the Trinity. This is an oversimplified explanation of a most profound mystery, the community of Persons in whose image we were created.

A man and a woman become one in marriage in a mysterious way that reveals the unity shared by the Father and the Son
(cf. Jn. 17:22-23). As the infinitely loving bond between the
Father and Son constitutes the Third Person of the Trinity, so
in a similar way a child embodies the love of a husband and
wife. The union of husband and wife is so profound that nine
months later the couple often have to give it a name when a
child is born! That is why the Church teaches that marriage is
a communion of life and love ordered toward the good of the
couple and the procreation and education of children, and that
there is an unbreakable bond between the love-giving and life-
giving aspects of marital love (cf., Catechism, nos. 1660, 2366).

God's Plan for Marriage

Some people mistakenly believe that the Church has
revised her teaching on homosexuality in recent years. On the
contrary, the Church has never taught that suffering from the
disorder of a homosexual inclination is in itself sinful. But the
Church has always taught that homosexual acts are "intrinsically" and "objectively" disordered (ibid., nos. 2357-58) and
"gravely contrary to chastity" (ibid., no. 2396). Further, having
an "innate impulse" (not "instinct") does not mean such a condition is normal or good, just as fallen man's inclination toward
sin is not normal or good.

God's wonderful plan for marriage allows husband and wife
to make up for each other's deficiencies and thereby complete
each other (cf. Gen. 2:18). This is known as complementarity, in
which the husband and wife become one through the mutual
giving and receiving of marital relations. This unity is reflected
in the crowning fruit of their union: children. Although some
married couples unfortunately cannot have children, they still
complete one another through the expression of mutual love.

In contrast, homosexual activity lacks complementarity,
but rather involves an illusory and vain attempt at communion. Under no circumstances can it be approved
(Catechism, no. 2357).

If we abandon the monogamous union of husband and wife
as the standard of marriage, there will be no logical argument
against "marriages" between homosexuals as well as between

polygamous heterosexuals. Government endorsement of homosexual "marriages" necessarily implies the acceptance of decadent polygamy and will only further undermine the moral fiber of our society.

As is the case with every dysfunction within the home, children suffer the most from the homosexual relationships of their parents. For some children, pain and confusion results when one parent leaves the other for a homosexual "union." Others adopted into a "family" of homosexual "parents" will probably never experience the example and natural beauty of a true marital relationship. Furthermore, homosexual unions often promote the development of reproductive technology to the exclusion of procreation according to God's design. Such technology makes the child a mere product of technology and denies the child the natural dignity and respect he deserves. Further, this technology denies the child his right to be born of a mother and father known to him (cf. Catechism, nos. 2376-77).

Teaching of Bishops

The U.S. Bishops' Committees on Marriage and Family and Domestic Policy likewise affirm this perennial teaching:

The Roman Catholic Church believes that marriage is a faithful, exclusive and lifelong union between one man and one woman joined as husband and wife in an intimate partnership of life and love. This union was established by God with its own proper laws. By reason of its very nature, therefore, marriage exists for the mutual love and support of the spouses and for the procreation and education of children. These two purposes, the unitive [love-giving] and the procreative [life-giving], are equal and inseparable. The institution of marriage has a very important relationship to the continuation of the human race, to the total development of the human person and to the dignity, stability, peace and prosperity of the family and of society.

Furthermore, we believe the natural institution of marriage has been blessed and elevated by Christ to the dignity of a sacrament. . . . Because they are married in the Lord, the spouses acquire a special relationship to each other and to society. Their love becomes a living image of the manner in which the Lord personally loves his people and is united with them. Living a Christian, sacramental marriage becomes their fundamental way of attaining salvation.

Because the marital relationship offers benefits unlike any other to persons, to society and to the church, we wish to make it clear that the institution of marriage, as the union of one man and one woman, must be preserved, protected and promoted in both private and public realms. At a time when family life is under significant stress, the principled defense of marriage is an urgent necessity for the well-being of children and families, and for the common good of society.

Thus, we oppose attempts to grant the legal status of marriage to a relationship between persons of the same sex. No same-sex union can realize the unique and full potential which the marital relationship expresses. For this reason, our opposition to "same-sex marriage" is not an instance of unjust discrimination or animosity toward homosexual persons. In fact, the Catholic Church teaches emphatically that individuals and society must respect the basic human dignity of all persons, including those with a homosexual orientation. Homosexual persons have a right to and deserve our respect, compassion, understanding and defense against bigotry, attacks and abuse.

We therefore urge Catholics and all our fellow citizens to commit themselves both to upholding the human dignity of every person and to upholding the distinct and irreplaceable community of marriage.[1]

---

[1] *Origins* (August 1, 1996), 133.

Courage to Be Chaste

If you know of someone who engages in homosexual activity, resist the temptation to act uncharitably. Depending on the circumstances, you may experience anger, frustration, repugnance, or any number of negative feelings toward the person. These feelings are normal, and of themselves are not sinful. However, we must love the sinner and hate the sin. We must not neglect any opportunity to witness in charity the truths of the faith. We must reach out to them in love to affirm their human dignity but not their sin. Most importantly, we must pray for them, that their hearts would be softened to accept their trial with courage and avoid any occasions of sin.

If you yourself struggle with the trial of homosexual inclinations, do not despair. The Church stands willing to strengthen you in your efforts to remain chaste. Through frequent reception of Confession and Holy Eucharist, and through the prayerful reading of Sacred Scripture, you can identify and avoid occasions of sin and root your life solidly in Christ. Additionally, there are many people who have the same struggle and who win. Several organizations within the Church assist people with homosexual tendencies to live according to the teachings of Christ. If you, or someone you know, is in need of assistance from one of these groups, do not hesitate to call Catholics United for the Faith's Information Services department toll-free at (800) MY-FAITH (693-2484). The staff will refer you to organizations that can help you.

Questions for Reflection
or Group Discussion

1. Why is marriage reserved only for a husband and a wife in a monogamous relationship? How would I explain this to someone who is not Christian? How would I explain this to someone with homosexual tendencies?

2. Do I understand the important distinction between loving the sinner and hating the sin? Is it possible to live this balance? Am I concerned about showing Christ-like compassion as well as not compromising the truth?

3. Do I truly strive to love homosexual persons, even when they are not at present willing to abandon an openly homosexual lifestyle? Do I understand that for most homosexuals, the inclination to engage in homosexual acts usually constitutes a trial (Catechism, no. 2358)? What can I do to help people who are going through such a trial? What can I do to help their family members?

RAISING TOMORROW'S SAINTS
The Catholic Education of Youth

What is Catholic education?

Catholic education recognizes that knowledge is at the service of man and must be directed toward the common good and the salvation of all. Such education requires training in the virtues and is rooted in the commandments of God. An education is truly Catholic to the degree an educator uses the educational experience to evangelize the students and form them in Christ.

To understand Catholic education, we do not need to understand a particular method of education. Rather, we must understand the nature of man, his relation to God, and his relation to others. In other words, we must start with the fundamental principles regarding the dignity and rights of the human person, and then apply them to the context of education. A method that builds on this foundation will reflect the mind of Christ and the discipline of His Church.

Purpose of Education

When we think of education, we typically think of formal training in certain basic or job-specific skills. Through education, a person learns to read, write, and calculate; he learns to use specific tools for a specific task; he furthers the advance of society through advances in technology and science. Although these are important results of education, these are not the primary purposes of education as set forth by the Church:

> All men of whatever race, condition, or age, in virtue of their dignity as human persons, have an inalienable right to education. This education should be suitable to the particular destiny of the individuals, adapted to their ability, sex, and national cul-

tural traditions, and should be conducive to fraternal relations with other nations in order to promote true unity and peace in the world. True education is directed towards the formation of the human person in view of his final end and the good of that society to which he belongs and in the duties of which he will, as an adult, have a share (GE 1, footnotes omitted).[1]

When we examine this statement, we find four important aspects of a true education.

1. *"All men of whatever race, condition, or age, in virtue of their dignity as human persons . . ."*

A proper education is a natural right of every person. Because every man is created in the image and likeness of God, he has a right, by the fact of his existence, to obtain an education suited to his existence.

2. *"This education should be suitable to the particular destiny of the individuals . . ."*

The existence of every man is suited to being formed in Christ. On Mount Sinai, God gave Moses the Ten Commandments (Ex. 20:2-17) as a light of understanding, so that we may know what must be done and what must be avoided. He gave these laws to bind all people, regardless of race, religion, or social class. They reflect the natural law written on the hearts of all men (cf. Rom. 2:15). They provide a minimum requirement for humanity (cf. VS 12). When he lives according to these laws, a man opens his heart to the grace of conversion. Faith and charity become the foundation of his life. He then is able to reach full maturity in Christ (cf. Eph. 4:11-14). These moral norms must permeate every educational experience, or the education falls short of the formation to which every man has a right.

---

[1] As a declaration, this Vatican II document is understood as a "policy statement" or application of previous documents and teachings on education. This text did not offer substantially new insights on the subject. Rather, it consolidated and applied the principles already taught by the Church.

3. *"True education is directed towards the formation of the human person . . ."*

"God's commandments show man the path of life and they lead to it" (VS 12). No man can follow God's commandments without reflecting on his relationship with God and his final destiny. A proper education will foster this reflection and encourage the pursuit of truth in the quest for knowledge of God. As affirmed by the Church, all men have the obligation to seek the truth and the right to live according to truth as they know it (canon 748; DH 2). A proper education, forming man into the humanity of Adam, will guide him to recognize the truth of Christ and allow him the opportunity to embrace it.

4. *"and the good of that society to which he belongs and in the duties of which he will, as an adult, have a share."*

God created man as a social being:

Life in society is not something accessory to man himself: through his dealings with others, through mutual service, and through fraternal dialogue, man develops all his talents and becomes able to rise to his destiny (GS 25).

To find fulfillment of purpose, one must live a life of faith and charity, first loving God and secondly loving one's neighbor for the love of God. In fulfilling these two great commandments, each person finds true meaning, and society finds prosperity and peace (cf. Deut. 6:4-9; Lev. 19:18; Mk. 9:29-31). In short, a proper education will teach man the sciences and arts, not for the sake of furthering knowledge, but rather to further knowledge for the sake of humanity. All must be ordered to the glory of God and the salvation of men.

Vatican II emphasized these concepts, not only in the above quotation, but throughout its *Declaration on Christian Education.* The sciences, arts, and technology should be tools through which each person develops physically, morally, spiritually, and intellectually (GE 1). In short, true education must direct a person to salvation and simultaneously promote unity and peace among all peoples; it must make him fully human.

From the Heart of the Church

Because an authentic education aimed at the purposes noted above points to Christ, education is not complete unless it is truly Catholic. In this regard, Vatican II clearly focuses on the knowledge of salvation and the life of grace:

> Such an education not only develops the maturity of the human person in the way we have described, but is especially directed towards ensuring that those who have been baptized, as they are gradually introduced to a knowledge of the mystery of salvation, become daily more appreciative of the gift of faith which they have received. They should learn to adore God the Father in spirit and in truth (Jn. 4:23), especially through the liturgy. They should be trained to live their own lives in the new self, justified and sanctified through the truth (Eph. 4:22-24) (GE 2).

Such an education allows the person to grow into manhood according to the mature measure of Christ (cf. Eph. 4:13) and devote himself to the building up of the Mystical Body. Moreover, aware of his calling, he should grow accustomed to giving witness to the hope that is in him (1 Pet. 3:15), and to promoting that Christian transformation of the world by which natural values, viewed in the full perspective of humanity as redeemed by Christ, may contribute to the good of society as a whole (cf. GE 2).

In the above passage, the Church identifies three "principal aims" that must permeate a truly Catholic educational experience:

1. *"that those who have been baptized, as they are gradually introduced to a knowledge of the mystery of salvation, become daily more appreciative of the gift of faith which they have received."*

Knowledge alone—even knowledge of God—does not save a man. In fact, the desire for knowledge tempted our first parents to sin (cf. Gen. 3:1-7). Man must direct knowledge by faith and, through knowledge, grow in faith. A Catholic education must be directed by the faith itself. Advances in the sciences and arts are necessarily seen in light of the eternal truths taught by the Church. Scientific theories that contradict the truths of faith, such as certain theories of evolution, must be rejected as false. In all things, knowledge must be presented in such a way as to draw the student to faith (cf. FR 15).

2. *"They should learn to adore God the Father in spirit and in truth (Jn. 4:23), especially through the liturgy."*

Adoration of God must be a principal aim of Catholic education. Our final destiny is to adore God forever in heaven. Through liturgical worship, the student is drawn into the eternal mysteries of God and sanctified in Christ. Equally important, because liturgical actions are not private actions, but celebrations of the Church herself, liturgical actions develop and strengthen unity among peoples and the good of society (SC 26-32). Liturgical worship, especially the celebration of the sacraments, provides the ordinary and necessary graces for the student to mature in the Christian life. It continually renews the student's faith, thus providing a firm foundation for all acquired knowledge.

3. *"They should be trained to live their own lives in the new self, justified and sanctified through the truth (Eph. 4:22-24)."*

In the Sermon on the Mount,

Jesus shows that the commandments must not be understood as a minimum limit not to be gone beyond, but rather as a path involving a moral and spiritual journey towards perfection, at the heart of which is love (cf. Col. 3:14) (VS 15).

This is the new standard of manhood, to become perfectly united to the Father in Christ through the power of the Spirit (cf. Jn. 17:21)—to become a living and personal fulfillment of the law of love.

The Catholic Educator

Authentic education primarily entails a formation in moral living and an invitation to knowledge of the truth. Specific knowledge and skill development are subordinate to an awareness of destiny and the obligations toward others. Catholic education fulfills the purposes of authentic education by enlightening the process with supernatural faith, adoration of God, and transformation of the person into the likeness of Christ.

The ideals of an authentic Catholic education will not be realized unless they take form through the experiences offered by an educator.[2] Unfortunately, much education today does not include proper formation or understanding of obligations toward others. Many educators emphasize knowledge for the sake of knowledge. It is not subordinate to faith. In many Catholic schools, religious education, adoration of God, and liturgical worship occur but do not permeate the educational environment. This allows errors concerning the nature of man and his destiny to influence the student's approach to the sciences and arts. Distrust between peoples is encouraged because of an overemphasis on the individual to the detriment of the common good.

The lay Catholic educator has tremendous influence over the students. Whether we look at schools in general or Catholic schools in particular, the influence of the laity is enormous. "For it is the lay teachers, and indeed all lay persons, believers or not, who will substantially determine whether or not a school realizes its aims and accomplishes its objectives."[3]

A Catholic educator has a serious obligation to saturate his teaching methods with respect for the rights of students and Christian charity. "It is in this context that the faith witness of the lay teacher becomes especially important."[4] He can only do

---

[2] Cf. Pope John Paul II, May 30, 1998 ad limina address to bishops from Illinois, Indiana, and Wisconsin, as reprinted in Lay Witness (March 1999), 44-45.
[3] Sacred Congregation for Catholic Education, Lay Catholics in Schools: Witnesses to Faith (1982), no. 1.
[4] Ibid., no. 32.

this if his own formation is proper and his faith strengthened by the Church and the sacraments of Christ.

Recognizing that many educational systems do not allow for an explicitly Catholic education to exist, the witness of Catholic educators by their way of life can nonetheless transform any educational setting into a Catholic experience. For the Catholic educator, "true education is not limited to the imparting of knowledge; it promotes human dignity and genuine human relationships, and prepares the way for opening oneself to the Truth that is Christ."[5]

Education is a tool of evangelization. To the degree an educator promotes human dignity and knowledge of the truth, the education is authentic. To the degree the educator forms the students into the likeness of Christ, the education is truly Catholic. Catholic educators would do well to saturate their lessons according to the principles given by Mother Church.

_____*SideBar*___

The Goal of Education

Men, created by God in His image and likeness and destined for Him Who is infinite perfection, realize today more than ever, amid the most exuberant material progress, the insufficiency of earthly goods to produce true happiness either for the individual or for the nations. And hence they feel more keenly in themselves the impulse toward a perfection that is higher, which impulse is implanted in their rational nature by the Creator Himself. This perfection they seek to acquire by means of education. But many of them with, it would seem, too great insistence on the etymological meaning of the word, pretend to draw education out of human nature itself and evolve it by its own unaided powers. Such easily fall into error, because, instead of fixing their gaze on

---

[5] *Ibid.*, no. 55.

God, first principle and last end of the whole universe, they fall back upon themselves, becoming attached exclusively to passing things of earth; and thus their restlessness will never cease till they direct their attention and their efforts to God, the goal of all perfection, according to the profound saying of Saint Augustine: "Thou didst create us, O Lord, for Thyself, and our heart is restless till it rests in Thee."

—Pope Pius XI, Encyclical Letter
On the Christian Education of Youth
Divini Illius Magistri (1930), quoting
Saint Augustine, *Confessions*, 1,1

Questions for Reflection or Group Discussion

1. The Church has traditionally taught that marriage is directed toward "the procreation and education of children for the worship of God." How does this discussion of Catholic education shed further light on this teaching?

2. What is the role of faith in the educational process? How does the Catholic faith affect studies such as math, science, and the arts?

3. Popes Paul VI and John Paul II have emphasized that people listen to teachers to the extent that they are *witnesses*. How do parents and others involved in Catholic education bear witness to Christ and His Church as they teach? How can I improve my own witness to the truths of the Catholic faith?

We Have But One Teacher, Jesus Christ
Catechesis in Our Time

What is the Church's view of catechesis?

Effective catechesis involves a deepening relationship with Jesus Christ and a growing knowledge of His Church's teachings. The goal is a vital relationship with Jesus Christ and His Mystical Body, the Church, so that the person in turn may bear effective witness to Christ in this life and share eternal happiness in heaven in the next. The achievement of this goal, which only occurs in cooperation with God's grace, may be furthered by sound catechisms, good priests and teachers, and dynamic parish programs. However, the most important component is the instruction and example given at home, the domestic Church, upon which everything else builds.

What Is Catechesis?

In his apostolic exhortation *Catechesi Tradendae* (Catechesis in Our Time), Pope John Paul II provides the following definition:

[C]atechesis is an education of children, young people and adults in the faith, which includes especially the teaching of Christian doctrine imparted, generally speaking, in an organic and systematic way, with a view to initiating the hearers into the fullness of Christian life (no. 18; cf. Catechism, no. 5).

As Bishop John J. Myers of Peoria, Illinois, wrote:

When we teach, we should first clearly present the church's teachings. People want to know and have a right to know what the church teaches and not merely to be presented with theological opinions, however clever (even our own). It is the

Gospel as entrusted to the church, which has the privileged assistance of the Holy Spirit and in the proclamation of which the Holy Spirit acts in a very profound manner.[1]

Catechesis involves nourishing the seed of faith that the person received at Baptism. Catechesis in one sense comes after evangelization, just as you get to know someone better only after you're introduced. Yet, the evangelical call to know and commit ourselves to Christ must permeate all catechesis. And this is particularly true today, where there are many who have been baptized, but have not yet committed their lives to Christ and are ignorant of His teachings.

The "springtime of faith" that Pope John Paul II envisions as the fruit of Vatican II and the Great Jubilee of the Year 2000 has a decidedly catechetical thrust. Catechism, no. 8 provides that "periods of renewal in the Church are also intense moments of catechesis." In his apostolic letter *Tertio Millennio Adveniente*, Pope John Paul II says that the Jubilee 2000 preparation provides an "opportune moment for a renewed appreciation of catechesis in its original meaning as the Apostles' teaching (Acts 2:42) about the person of Jesus Christ and His mystery of salvation" (no. 42). It seems appropriate, then, to do everything we can now to promote effective catechesis.

The principal documents on this subject, besides Scripture and the Catechism, are Pope John Paul II's apostolic exhortation *Catechesi Tradendae* (CT), the 1971 *General Catechetical Directory* (GCD), the 1997 *General Directory for Catechesis* (GDC), and the 1979 *National* (i.e., U.S.) *Catechetical Directory* (NCD).

Who Is Communicated?

[A]t the heart of catechesis we find, in essence, a Person, the Person of Jesus of Nazareth. . . . [Therefore,] [t]he primary and essential object of catechesis is . . . to reveal in the Person of

---

[1] Most Rev. John J. Myers, "On Sharing Difficult Truths," *Origins* (February 27, 1997), vol. 26, 592.

Christ the whole of God's eternal design reaching fulfilment in that Person. . . . Accordingly, the definitive aim of cate-chesis is to put people not only in touch but in communion, in intimacy, with Jesus Christ: only he can lead us to the love of the Father in the Spirit and make us share in the life of the Holy Trinity (CT 5; cf. Catechism, no. 425).

Catechesis must aim to put people in communion with Jesus Christ (CT 5), and thus should be centered on Christ, the "alpha and omega" of our faith (Rev. 22:13). It also follows that Christ's teaching, and not the opinions or agendas of the cat-echist, must be communicated (CT 6, 52). Pope John Paul II reminds catechists to apply to themselves the mysterious words of Jesus: "My teaching is not mine, but his who sent me" (Jn. 7:16). Catechists, like Saint John the Baptist, must humbly decrease, so that God's own Word, which is "living and active" (Heb. 4:12), may increase and penetrate people's hearts (cf. Jn. 3:30).

If catechesis were only abstract teaching, then the goal would be imparting knowledge. But catechesis is much more! It is the formation of effective Catholics. Therefore, the goal of the catechist must always be to set hearts aflame for Christ: "Did not our hearts burn within us while he talked to us on the road, while he opened to us the scriptures?" (Lk. 24:32).

Who Communicates?

The work of catechesis is a collaborative effort of the People of God, yet the decisive role of parents is singled out in Church documents. For example, canon 774 §2 provides that "[p]arents above others are obliged to form their children in the faith and practice of the Christian life by word and example."

Pope John Paul II teaches that "[t]he family's catechetical activity has a special character, which is in a sense irreplace-able" (CT 68). He then points out that this principle has been affirmed by the Church for centuries, and received particular emphasis at Vatican II.

The central document of Vatican II, *Lumen Gentium* (Dogmatic Constitution on the Church), explains: "In what might be regarded as the domestic Church, the parents, by word and example, are the first heralds of the faith with regard to their children" (no. 11). And then in *Gravissimum Educationis* (Decree on Christian Education), this point is further clarified:

> As it is the parents who have given life to their children, on them lies the *gravest obligation of educating their family.* They must therefore be recognized as being primarily and principally responsible for their education. *The role of parents in education is of such importance that it is almost impossible to provide an adequate substitute.* . . . It is therefore above all in the Christian family, inspired by the grace and the responsibility of the sacrament of matrimony, that children should be taught to know and worship God and to love their neighbor, in accordance with the faith which they have received in earliest infancy in the sacrament of Baptism (GE 3, footnote omitted, emphasis added).

Parents may be assisted in their task by other catechists, be they clergy, religious, or laity. Their duty is not only to impart authentic Church teaching, but also to be "living witnesses," to manifest in their lives what they are communicating to the children (GCD 35; cf. 1 Thess. 2:8). Children should be exposed to good role models whenever possible, such as through introduction to saints' lives, but also through interaction with outstanding Catholic men and women. The point is that *all of us*—and especially children—need to see how the Gospel is changing people's lives.

How Communicated?

Our sacred religion hinges on the revelation of Jesus Christ, who is "the way, and the truth, and the life" (Jn. 14:6). We're not born with the knowledge of Christ, nor will we naturally come to a knowledge of Him unless He is proclaimed to us. We need to be taught the truths of our faith. As the Ethiopian eunuch replied to Philip, after being asked if he understood the Scripture he was reading, "How can I, unless some one guides me?" (Acts 8:31).

Life experiences may demonstrate to us our need for Christ and His Church. Further, once the faith is accepted and learned, it may inform our experiences. However, "no one can arrive at the whole truth on the basis solely of some simple private experience, that is to say, without an adequate explanation of Christ, who is 'the way, and the truth, and the life'" (CT 22, quoting Jn. 14:6).

In presenting the Catholic faith, a catechist must communicate the truth faithfully and in a manner adapted to the person's age and culture (cf. 1 Cor. 9:22). The teacher should manifest a "dynamic orthodoxy." The teaching should be *dynamic*, since "routine, with its refusal to accept any change" is "dangerous for catechesis" and "leads to stagnation, lethargy, and eventual paralysis" (CT 17). Yet the teaching must always be *orthodox*, faithfully presenting what the Church teaches "in all its rigor and vigor" (CT 30). The catechist must reject improvisation as "equally dangerous" and the cause of "confusion" and the "destruction of unity" (CT 17).

Effective catechesis must be complete and systematic. Even when dealing with young children, catechesis should reveal, in an elementary way, *all* the principal mysteries of the faith in a way that allows the child to see how the various teachings form an organic whole, centered on Christ (GCD 38-39, 118; NCD 47, 176; CT 30, 31, 37, 49; GDC 97-100). It must promote a complete Christian initiation (CT 21), so that all the dimensions of the Christian life (e.g., liturgy, morality, social justice, etc.) are integrated.

Catechetical programs must be free from private opinion, ideology, or agenda, and present the unadulterated deposit of faith with conviction (e.g., CT 52, 61; Catechism, nos. 85-87, 890, 2039). The focus must be on essentials, and not on disputed theological points. In other words, catechetical tools must be at the service of the teaching Church, following the sure guidance of the Magisterium.

Memorization plays an important role in catechesis. The Holy Father encourages the memorization of "the words of Jesus, of important Bible passages, of the Ten Commandments, of the formulas of the profession of faith [i.e., Creeds], of the liturgical texts, of the essential prayers, of key doctrinal ideas, etc.," calling this "a real need" in the Church today (CT 55). He further explains:

The blossoms . . . of faith and piety do not grow in the desert
places of a memory-less catechesis. What is essential is that
the texts that are memorized must at the same time be taken
in and gradually understood in depth, in order to become a
source of Christian life on the personal and community
level (*ibid.*).

The goal of all catechetical activity is the conversion of
hearts, so that the person may respond to the Lord's call with
heroic generosity. Young people particularly need to be challenged
to sanctity today. The desire to make the Gospel accessible
to youth is misguided if the call to repent and follow Jesus
(cf. Mk. 1:15) is in any way watered down.

When the young man asked Jesus, "[W]hat good deed must
I do, to obtain eternal life?" (Mt. 19:16), Jesus looked at him
with love and personally invited the young man to follow Him
without reserve (Mt. 19:21; cf. Jn. 14:6).

What Is to Be Taught?

Any sound catechetical program will provide an effective
treatment of the following topics, since they are the principal
elements of the Christian message:

1. The Trinitarian mystery; three Persons in one God: Father,
   Son, and Holy Spirit.

2. Creation of the world from nothing; existence of angels;
   special creation of man.

3. Jesus Christ as the Son of God, true God and true man.

4. Christ as Savior and Redeemer of the world, who through
   His death and Resurrection offers eternal life to all men
   and women.

5. Presence of the Holy Spirit as the Lord and giver of life; His
   special presence in the Church, continuing Christ's work
   in the world.

6. The Catholic Church as founded by Christ, possessing the deposit of faith, the sacraments, the ministries inherited from the apostles, and the fullness of the ordinary means of salvation for all people.

7. The Church as being "in" the world, but not "of" the world, and never conforming to it; her Christ-given mission to bring the message of salvation to all, with heaven, the salvific goal she shares with all people, kept always in view.

8. The Pope and the bishops as having the office of teaching, sanctifying, and governing the Church, and enjoying the gift of infallibility in guiding the Church when they exercise supreme teaching authority in matters of faith and morals, whether through the ordinary Magisterium (definitive teaching of the Pope and the bishops in union with him around the world), or through the extraordinary Magisterium: (a) through a formal, conciliar definition as at the Council of Trent (cf. LG 25) or (b) through an *ex cathedra* pronouncement of the Pope, such as Mary's Immaculate Conception; submission to the Magisterium is required even with respect to non-*ex cathedra* teachings.

9. The sacraments, as signifying the gift of grace and the faith of the Christian community, and as the actions of Christ from whom they receive their power.

10. The Eucharist as the center and heart of Christian life, a commemoration and re-presentation of Christ's one and only sacrifice on the Cross. Transubstantiation and the Real and abiding Presence of Christ in the Blessed Sacrament.

11. Effect of original sin as arising from the personal sin of one man at the dawn of history through the urging of the devil; personal sin as the rejection of God's commands or love, involving exterior or interior acts contrary to God's law; distinction between mortal and venial sin.

12. The doctrine of grace and the means of obtaining it.

13. The fact that human freedom must be exercised in confomity with moral law, i.e., the natural law, the Ten Commandments, and the teachings of the Church.

14. The Blessed Ever-Virgin Mary, who occupies in the Holy Church the place which is highest after Christ; immaculately conceived and gloriously assumed into heaven, Mother of God and Mother of the Church.

15. The fact that Christians draw inspiration from the heroic example of Mary and the saints, look for fellowship in their communion, and seek their intercession before God.

16. Death, judgment (individual and general), heaven, hell, and purgatory, and the resurrection of the body.

Questions for Reflection
or Group Discussion

1. Pope John Paul II says that the catechesis of adults is "a concern imposed with vigor and urgency by present experiences throughout the world," and that it is the "principal" form of catechesis (CT 43). What can I do to deepen my own knowledge of the Catholic faith and deepen my relationship with Christ and His Church?

2. (For parents) Read Catechism, no. 2226. How can I make my home more fully a "domestic Church" where my children may receive a sound formation in the Catholic faith?

3. Catechesis necessarily involves teaching all the truths of the Catholic faith. What else does it entail? What is the relationship between evangelization and catechesis? (See Catechism, nos. 426-29.)

Chapter 16

WHERE DO WE GO WRONG?
Top Ten Errors in Catechesis Today

What are the most common problems with some modern cate-chetical resources?

The *Catechism of the Catholic Church* is the ultimate standard by which all catechetical resources should be evaluated. We are blessed to have in our day such a comprehensive and useful resource to help us present our faith to others. However, the Catechism is not meant to replace all of the various catechisms that are on the market, but rather to encourage and assist in the updating of old series and the writing of new ones that faithfully present Catholic doctrine.

All catechetical programs must be centered in Christ and His teachings. These divinely revealed truths, known as the "deposit of faith," are preserved and handed down to each successive generation through Scripture, Tradition, and the Magisterium (teaching office) of the Church (Catechism, nos. 84-87, 888-92). In teaching the faith, then, a catechetical program must be based on God's own revealed truth. Scripture and Tradition should not be downplayed at the expense of "personal reflection." Unfortunately, it is at this foundational level where many catechetical programs show their first signs of weakness. In some cases, God has been depicted as man's dialogue partner and, in others, Scripture has become nothing more than a reflection of "shared faith experience."

It is, of course, very important that every person have a living, personal faith that manifests itself in the way the person lives (cf. CT 22). However, methods that value personal experience over the objective content of the Catholic faith contribute to many of the doctrinal errors we encounter today. Christ and His teachings change us (this process is called *conversion*); we do not change Christ and His teachings according to our preferences or inclinations.

Many modern catechisms approach God, not through what He has revealed through Scripture and Tradition, but through personal experience. This approach severely limits what can be taught. In an oral report delivered to the National Conference of Catholic Bishops (NCCB) on June 19, 1997, Archbishop Daniel Buechlein pointed out again and again that human action, human initiative, and human experience are commonly overemphasized in some catechetical materials, while the power and divinity of God seem to be undermined. These errors could be more effectively addressed if the approach were corrected. As Pope John Paul II has said,

> No one can arrive at the whole truth on the basis solely of some simple private experience, that is to say, without an adequate explanation of the message of Christ, who is "the way, and the truth, and the life" (Jn. 14:6) (CT 22).

The Church is not opposed to experience, but she wants us to experience Jesus Christ in all of His truth and power.

All catechisms should strive to present true Christian teaching. Unfortunately, many of these resources fall short in several important areas.

As authentic teachers of the Catholic faith, bishops have a vital role to play in catechesis (cf. LG 25; Catechism, no. 888). Therefore, in evaluating a particular catechetical resource, it is helpful to refer to the ten problem areas identified by Archbishop Buechlein, the chairman of the U.S. Bishops' Ad Hoc Committee to Oversee the Use of the Catechism, in his 1997 report. These problem areas are identified below, with each containing a "things to look for" section which lists a few common ways the problems are manifested in current textbooks.

1. The Trinity: Matthew 28:18-20

God has revealed Himself as a community of Persons (Gen. 1:26), as one God in three Persons: Father, Son, and Holy Spirit. "The mystery of the Most Holy Trinity is the central mystery of [the] Christian faith" (Catechism, no. 234; GDC 99). Jesus is God (Jn. 1:14; 8:58), the Father is God

(Ex. 4:13-14; 20:2-3), and so is the Holy Spirit (Gen. 1:1; Joel 2:28-32; Acts 1:8, 2:1-4). There is a distinction of Persons in the Trinity, though each totally possesses one divine nature (cf. Jn. 17:22-23).

The Sign of the Cross, often the first prayer taught to children, attests to the centrality of this mystery of the faith. Often, unfortunately, this essential mystery is not adequately presented in catechetical texts. God has revealed that He is one God in a Trinity of Persons. Jesus Himself revealed the personal nature of the Trinity when He called upon God as His Father. Each of the three Persons of the Trinity has a specific role in our salvation. Therefore, it is often necessary to refer to one or more of the Persons of the Trinity by their proper name. Catechetical resources often downplay the personal character of the Trinity in an effort to be more "inclusive." Frequently, texts will abandon the vocabulary of Revelation and the Church by avoiding the use of "Father" and "Son" for the First and Second Persons of the Trinity.

Things to look for: The use of substitute words, such as "Parent God" for God the Father or the over-repetition of "God" when the context calls for "Father" or "God the Father"; also the use of "God" or "Creator/Redeemer/Sanctifier" instead of the divinely revealed masculine proper names "Father," "Son," or "Holy Spirit," or biblically based pronouns "He" or "Him."

2. Christ: John 1:14

Jesus Christ "came from God" (Jn. 13:3), "descended from heaven" (Jn. 3:13), and came "in the flesh" (1 Jn. 4:2). He is the Anointed One (Mt. 16:16), the Son of God (Acts 9:20), the incarnate Word of God (Jn 1:1, 14), both fully man and fully divine. As He told the Jews, "before Abraham was, I am" (Jn. 8:58; cf. Ex. 4:11-12).

The General Directory for Catechesis (GDC), approved by Pope John Paul II in 1997, teaches that

[t]he message centered on the person of Jesus Christ (*christocentricity*), by its inherent dynamic, introduces the trinitarian dimension of the same message. . . . Thus what must charac-

terize the message transmitted by catechesis is, above all, its "christocentricity" (GDC 97-98; cf. CT 5-6).

The Sign of the Cross not only attests to the central importance of the Trinity, but also to the salvation which came through Jesus by way of the Cross. Jesus Christ is the fulfillment of God's plan for all of humanity. Saint Paul writes that in the fullness of time, "God sent forth his Son, born of a woman, born under the law, to redeem those who were under the law, so that we might receive adoption as sons" (Gal. 4:4-5). Scripture further teaches that "there is salvation in no one else" (Acts 4:12). Thus, two essential truths about Christ must be affirmed and highly emphasized in any catechism: His divinity and the centrality of His becoming man in salvation history.

Things to look for: Overemphasizing Jesus the teacher, model, friend, or brother to the neglect of Jesus the Savior; underemphasizing the divinity of Jesus Christ or equating divinity with being "distant and unreal," while presenting Jesus Christ in mostly human and naturalistic terms; asserting that Jesus, despite being God, was ignorant about anything or many things, including His own identity and mission; and downplaying the importance of the Incarnation as the fulfillment of Old Testament prophecy.

3. The Church: Matthew 16:18

The Church was founded by Jesus Christ (Mt. 16:16-19) and built on the foundation of the apostles to continue Christ's mission in the world (LG 5, 8). The Church, which is the "pillar and bulwark of the truth" (1 Tim. 3:15), has sought the conversion of the world since apostolic times. This has been accomplished through the guidance of the Holy Spirit (Jn. 16:13), the proclamation of God's Word (Is. 55:10-11), the celebration of the sacraments, and the teaching office of the apostles. The Church is one, holy, catholic, and apostolic (Nicene Creed; Catechism, nos. 820, 867-68; Rev. 21:14), animated by the Spirit, with "one Lord, one faith, one baptism, one God and Father of us all, who is above all and through all and in all" (Eph. 4:4-6).

The teaching authority known as the Magisterium is constituted by the successors of Peter and the apostles: the Pope and the bishops in union with him (Catechism, nos. 84-87; cf. Lk. 10:16; Mt. 18:18; Eph. 4:11). The Magisterium has the authority to teach and govern the faithful in the name of Jesus Christ (Catechism, nos. 888-96). Thus, Catholic beliefs and magisterial teachings are to be understood as coming from the Church that Christ founded. What we believe is what Christ teaches.

Things to look for: Not clearly presenting the Church as founded by Christ, with His continuing guidance and mission in the world (Mt. 28:18-20); de-emphasis of the Church's teaching function, its apostolic nature, the role of the hierarchy, and the leadership role of bishops and priests as teachers of the Word of God; playing the Church's universality and diversity against its essential unity; asserting incorrectly that teachings on sexual morality such as the indissolubility of marriage, contraception, abortion, etc., are not infallible; questioning the whole concept of infallibility and asserting that the consensus of Catholics or theologians determines the status of any teaching. In reality, the *sensus fidelium* (the sense of the faithful) always implies that the faithful are just that, faithful to the Magisterium (LG 12).

4. Christian Anthropology: Genesis 1:26-28
As we are led by the Spirit of God, we are given the right to be called sons and daughters of God (Rom. 8:14-17).

The human person is by nature religious (Rom. 2:14-16). God has made us, redeemed us, and called us to communion with Him (cf. 2 Pet. 1:4). This truth, at the very minimum, obliges man in justice to give to God what is due Him. Furthermore, the soul of man is spiritual by nature. As Saint Augustine so beautifully wrote, "Our heart is restless until it rests in [God]."[1] Thus, any study of the nature and end of man must begin and end with his vocation to sanctity and his relationship to his Creator and Lord (cf. Catechism, nos. 1716-29).

---

[1] *The Confessions of St. Augustine* (Garden City, NY: Image Books, 1960) trans. by J.K. Ryan, 43.

Things to look for: Reducing the human person to the merely material; the common omission that it was in Christ that we were created in the image and likeness of God, and that Christ has restored to us the divine image and likeness which has been defiled by sin; and the implication that the human person is the first principle and final end of his or her own existence.

5. God's Initiative: John 15:16

God created the world (Gen. 1-2) and has redeemed man through the Paschal Mystery of His Son, that is, Jesus' death and Resurrection (see problem area no. 2, above). The Book of Proverbs affirms God's omnipotence: "Many are the plans in the mind of man, but it is the purpose of the Lord that will be established" (Prov. 19:21).

God not only created the world, He also cares for it as a good father cares for his family. God is actively involved in the lives of all persons, giving them grace upon grace to enable them to do good (Jn. 1:16) and avoid evil. Yet these days, many catechetical series overemphasize the action of man to the point that it appears to the reader that human initiative is the prerequisite for divine assistance. This could not be further from the truth. The truth is that human action is intended to follow upon God's action and initiative in the world. We can do nothing without God, who created us out of nothing and holds us in existence (Catechism, no. 320).

Things to look for: God's initiative appears subordinate to human experience and human action.

6. Grace: Romans 8:14-17

By definition, grace is "the free and undeserved help that God gives us to respond to his call to become . . . partakers of the divine nature and of eternal life" (Catechism, no. 1996; cf. 2 Pet. 1:4).

> You did not receive the spirit of slavery . . . but . . . the spirit of sonship. When we cry, "Abba! Father!" It is the Spirit himself bearing witness with our spirit that we are children of God, and if children, then heirs, heirs of God and fellow heirs

with Christ, provided we suffer with him in order that we may also be glorified with him (Rom. 8:15-17).

Grace is a supernatural gift, meaning it comes solely from God and depends entirely on God's initiative (Catechism, no. 1998). The U.S. bishops have noted that many popular catechisms define grace simply as God's love for us, and thus these texts generally fail to treat grace as an unmerited gift from God that enables us to identify ourselves as His adopted sons and daughters and to share more fully in His life. Many catechisms are also weak on their treatment of the sacramental graces.

Things to look for: Grace defined simply as God's love; overemphasis on human effort in obtaining grace.

7. Sacraments: Ephesians 3:9-10

The sacraments were instituted by Christ as necessary for salvation (cf. Catechism, nos. 1114, 1129). Christ directs the Church in dispensing these mysteries (Eph. 3:9-10). Through His Paschal Mystery, Christ became the "source of eternal salvation" (Heb. 5:5-10). At the Mass, in which Christ exercises His role as priest, His one paschal sacrifice is re-presented sacramentally. It is also because of His one death and Resurrection, Archbishop Buechlein notes, that all the other sacraments are made possible (cf. 1 Cor. 15:12-23). Given God's freely chosen eternal plan of salvation, Christ cannot forgive sins, enable us to partake of His Body and Blood and divine nature, and empower priests to celebrate the sacraments without first conquering sin and death Himself (Rom. 5:12-21; 11:25-27).

The sacraments are the usual means by which God communicates His grace to us. Thus, we say that God communicates His divine life to us through what we call the "sacramental economy." The sacramental economy, consisting principally of the sacred liturgy and the seven sacraments of the Catholic faith, is the means by which God establishes, maintains, supports, nourishes, and loves His family, the Church. Each sacrament draws its power from the timeless event of the Paschal Mystery, for Christ's redemptive sacrifice transcends history. The new life of the Resurrection is then shared by the faithful through the power of the Holy Spirit. Finally, the grace of the sacraments is truly communicated through the very signs that signify the supernatural realities.

Archbishop Buechlein reported that in some catechetical texts, "the sacraments are often presented as important events in human life of which God becomes a part, rather than as effective signs of divine life in which humans participate." The power of the sacraments is obscured when catechetical texts manifest a deficient understanding of the divine action and overlook the graced transformation at the heart of the sacraments.

Things to look for: Sacraments presented as being representative of events in human life of which God becomes a part; deficient treatment of the importance of the Paschal Mystery in the sacramental economy; downplaying or deficient presentation of the Sacrament of Holy Orders and the priesthood in general; inadequate explanation of Christ's Real Presence in the Eucharist; Baptism treated as a rite that merely symbolizes our entry into the community.

8. Original Sin: Romans 3:23

Just as we are by nature religious, we are also by nature sinful. Saint Paul writes in his Letter to the Romans, "Therefore as sin came into the world through one man and death through sin, and so death spread to all men because all men sinned" (5:12). This writing is echoed in the teachings of the Council of Trent, which taught that original sin is transmitted by human nature and is present in each person. Pope Paul VI explained:

> [O]n account of the original offense committed by him . . . fallen human nature is deprived of the economy of grace which it formerly enjoyed. It is wounded in its natural powers and subjected to the dominion of death which is transmitted to all men.[2]

---

[2] Pope Paul VI, *The Creed of the People of God* (1968), no. 16, as reprinted in Austin Flannery, O.P., ed., *Vatican Council II: More Post Conciliar Documents* (Collegeville, MN: The Liturgical Press, 1982), 391; cf. Catechism, no. 418.

But Christ has conquered sin: "For as by one man's disobedience many were made sinners, so by one man's obedience many will be made righteous" (Rom. 5:19).

Unfortunately, many catechism series do not deal appropriately with these teachings on original sin. Part of this is the result of the experience-based methodology, which admits the goodness—but not the fallenness—of mankind. Many lack basic explanations fundamental to our understanding of the nature of sin and its effects on our life. The Catechism states that by tampering with the revelation of original sin, we undermine the mystery of Christ (no. 389). In addition to this difficulty, some texts frequently do not note that the dogma of original sin informs other doctrines, like grace, Baptism, and redemption.

Things to look for: De-emphasis of the sinful nature of all mankind; downplaying Christ's role as necessary for our salvation; and a view that stresses sincerity and knowledge without supernatural grace and divine assistance.

9. Christian Moral Life: Matthew 19:16

In living the life of Christ, we are called to partake of His nature (2 Pet. 1:4) and imitate Him in all things, taking up our cross daily (Mt. 16:24-26) and laying down our lives for Him (Jn. 15:13). Impoverished catechisms present the moral life as so many rules and regulations, or opt for an experience-based treatment that encourages students to decide for themselves what is right or wrong based on their own feelings and experiences.

For decades now, our society has opted for the wide and easy path (Mt. 7:13-14) and exalted the self as the primary judge of morality (cf. Rom. 1:18-32). The fruit of this social experiment is all too evident. Some catechisms used today reject or downplay the reality of mortal sin. In contrast, Scripture teaches that unrepented mortal sins bring eternal death (1 Cor. 6:9-11; 1 Jn. 5:16-19). The Catholic Church proclaims that the source of morality is found in God's revealed law, as taught by the Church, and is grounded in natural law (Rom. 1:18-25; 2:14-16). This deficiency in understanding is directly related to poor teaching on original sin. The Catechism provides the critically important insight that "[i]gnorance of the fact that man has a wounded nature inclined to evil gives rise to serious errors in the areas of education, politics, social action, and morals" (no. 407). One would hope that as some of the other problematic areas are remedied, this area would be naturally corrected.

Many catechisms do not present the binding force of the Church's moral teaching. In addition, there is a lack of explanation as far as conscience formation is concerned. The Church clearly teaches that a properly formed conscience must reject the temptation to prefer one's private inclinations over the authoritative teaching of the Church (cf. Catechism, nos. 1783, 2039). "Deep within his conscience man discovers a law which he has not laid upon himself but which he must obey. . . . For man has in his heart a law inscribed by God" (GS 16). The authority of the Church in areas of morals must be stressed as well as the importance of our submission to this authority.

Things to look for: Treatment of the self as the primary and/or definitive source of morality; de-emphasis of the authority of the Church.

10. Last Things: Matthew 16:26

Jesus speaks of a final judgment in which the sheep will be separated from the goats, the good from the evil, His disciples from those who reject His kingdom (Mt. 25:31-46). There is death, the first of the last things, after which comes judgment, the second (Heb. 9:27). Each person who is judged will have everlasting joy in heaven or everlasting anguish in hell (Mt. 25:46). Those who are unclean (Rev. 21:27) must be prepared for eternal communion with the Trinity through the fiery purification of God's love (1 Cor. 3:15) in purgatory (Catechism, nos. 1030-32).

The whole of the Christian life can be characterized as a preparation for a holy death. At death, if one's soul is in a state of sanctifying grace, it will be assured a heavenly reward for all eternity upon the completion of any needed purification and perfection. However, those who die in a state of mortal sin will suffer eternal punishment. Therefore, the truth about death and what happens to each person after death is extremely important. This truth, which is known as the doctrine of the "last things" or eschatology, concerns death, judgment, heaven, hell, and purgatory.

Things to look for: A naïve assumption that all souls are "in a better place" upon death; certitude of the departed soul's heavenly residence; the omission of any discussion of either the particular or general judgment or the reality of hell; the de-emphasis of the beatific vision of heaven; the emphasis on the ability to realize the kingdom of God in this world; the neglect of the transcendent, trans-temporal and trans-historical nature of the kingdom; poor treatment of the relationship of morality and the sacraments to our eternal destiny.

As faithful Catholics, we should rejoice in the teachings of Jesus Christ. The Catholic Church has been given to us so that we may experience the abundant life Christ offers (Jn. 10:10). All of the Church's teachings are to be accepted if we desire to live a life of faith in Jesus (Catechism, no. 1814).

Questions for Reflection
or Group Discussion

1. Read Catechism, no. 24 and, if available, section 3 of Pope John Paul II's apostolic constitution *Fidei Depositum* (Deposit of Faith), which appears at the beginning of most versions of the Catechism. Why does the Church encourage the publication of various catechetical programs in addition to the *Catechism of the Catholic Church?*

2. (For parents) What practical steps can I take when my child's catechetical program doesn't teach the Catholic faith in its fullness? What other catechetical materials can I use to supplement my child's religious education?

3. A personal relationship with Jesus Christ lived out in the heart of the Church is the goal of every catechist. What is the problem with placing too much emphasis on personal experience? What is the problem with de-emphasizing the role of experience?

Chapter 17

PURE BIOLOGY?
Effective Chastity Education

How can parents determine whether a particular "sex education" program will effectively teach their children the virtue of chastity?

One of the most challenging issues parents encounter today is teaching their children the true meaning of sexuality. How can parents evaluate whether a chastity program will help them form their children in virtue?

To determine whether such a program is faithfully and effectively assisting the parents, there are six useful questions, based on a wealth of Church teaching on the subject, that should be asked. These questions should be considered particularly in light of *The Truth and Meaning of Human Sexuality: Guidelines for Education Within the Family* (TMHS), published in late 1995 by the Pontifical Council for the Family.

1. Does the program itself call for strong parental involvement? Does it respect the rights of both the parents and the child? (TMHS 113, 120, 145).

2. Is the program designed for use in a coeducational setting? Trying to teach chastity in such a setting violates the child's privacy and modesty, and simply is counterproductive (TMHS 127).

3. Does the program respect the different phases of development? In particular, does the program violate the child's years of innocence (i.e., "latency" or pre-puberty stage) by presenting explicit, biological information prematurely? (TMHS 64, 65, 75, 78, 83).

4. Does the program recognize that the primary obstacle to chastity is not ignorance but sin? Does the program seek to form saints or to inform sinners? (TMHS 122-23; Catechism, no. 407).

5. Does the program include graphic illustrations or have other aspects that offend modesty and chastity? (TMHS 126, 127, 133, 139, 143).

6. Are the Church's moral teachings believed and communicated by the teacher? Are safeguards in place to ensure that the teacher does not dissent from Church teaching in sensitive marriage and family issues? (TMHS 116, 117, 120, 135, 145).

The implementation of sex education programs in Catholic schools throughout the country is a complex, divisive issue in the Church in our time. Since parents are the first and most important educators of their children, it is essential that they understand the teachings of Christ and His Church as they bear on this difficult issue.

Whose Responsibility Is It?

It is clear from Vatican II that parents are primarily and principally responsible for the education of their children. In fact, in reaffirming this constant Church teaching, the Council provided that "[t]he role of parents in education is of such importance that it is almost impossible to provide an adequate substitute" (GE 3).

The parents' primary role with respect to education in marital love in particular is repeatedly confirmed by papal and conciliar teachings. Note, for example, the following passage from Vatican II:

> It is imperative to give suitable and timely instruction to young people, *above all in the heart of their own families*, about the dignity of married love, its role and its exercise; in this way they will be able to engage in honorable courtship and enter upon [a] marriage of their own (GS 49, emphasis added).

Conversely, the Church recognizes that parents may call upon the Church, and especially the Catholic school, to assist in the work of sex education. However, this assistance may not in any way usurp the primary role of the parents:

> Sex education, which is a basic right and duty of parents, must always be carried out under their attentive guidance, whether at home or in educational centers chosen and controlled by them. In this regard, the Church reaffirms the law of subsidiarity, which the school is bound to observe when it cooperates in sex education, by entering into the same spirit that animates the parents (FC 37).[1]

In *The Truth and Meaning of Human Sexuality*, the Pontifical Council for the Family affirms the primary and fundamental role of parents in chastity education. "Other educators can assist in this task, but they can only take the place of parents for serious reasons of physical or moral incapacity" (TMHS 23). As Pope Pius XI wrote earlier this century:

> In this extremely delicate matter, if, all things considered, some private instruction is found necessary and opportune, from those who hold from God the mission to teach and who are [in] the grace of state, every precaution must be taken. Such precautions are well known in traditional Christian education. . . .[2]

The Truth and Meaning of Human Sexuality is full of references affirming parents as the primary educators of their children, particularly on matters such as chastity formation (note especially nos. 23, 41, 47, 145, 146, 148; cf. Catechism, nos. 2221-31).

The role of the Catholic school is subordinate, then, to that of the parents, and subject to the parents' attentive guidance

---

[1] See also Pope John Paul II, *Letter to Families*, Vatican translation (Boston: St. Paul Books & Media, 1994), no. 16.

[2] Pope Pius XI, Encyclical Letter On the Christian Education of Youth *Divini Illius Magistri* (1930), no. 59.

and control. Parents should be empowered to fulfill their duties, and not pressured to delegate them.

> Everyone must observe the right order of cooperation and collaboration between parents and those who can help them in their task. It is clear that the assistance of others must be given first and foremost to parents rather than to their children (TMHS 145).

On the one hand, Catholic educators are too frequently faced with children whose parents have wrongly abdicated personal responsibility for their children's education. On the other hand, Catholic parents who take seriously their duties feel as though their "basic right" to educate their children is trampled upon by the way many sex education programs are implemented. This latter difficulty is admittedly worsened by differences over the appropriateness of the program's subject matter and teaching methods. However, regardless of the merits of a particular program, the parents' primary role must be accepted by parents and respected and fostered by educators. This perspective assuredly points to a proactive, parent-based approach. Parents may need assistance, but not replacement.

Concretely, "the rights of parents are violated if their children are compelled to attend classes which are not in agreement with the religious beliefs of the parents. . ." (DH 5). A program that is faithful to Church teaching will provide parents the liberty to decide—without coercion or negative repercussions—whether their children will participate (TMHS 117, 120). As Cardinal Gagnon, then President of the Pontifical Council for the Family, commented in 1990:

> It may well be that a particular bishop or even a conference of bishops judges that a sex education course be offered in the Catholic school. . . . However, . . . no ecclesiastical or civil authority may legitimately mandate that every pupil in the school take such a course, even though this course may seem to them to be completely beneficial to the children. . . . [If it] is not in agreement with the moral

and religious convictions of certain parents, it is the right of these parents, and the obligation of the Catholic school to respect this right, to have their children excused from the sex education class.[3]

The Human Condition

As a result of original sin, we as a human family have lost our friendship with God and thereby are in need of salvation, which is offered to all through Jesus Christ. Through Baptism, our children have indeed become "new creations" (2 Cor. 5:17). However, a key truth of faith that is readily confirmed by our experience is that even the baptized retain an inclination to sin called *concupiscence*, which at root refers to the weakened, frail state of our human nature. This weakness and division we find in ourselves is described by Saint Paul in Romans 7:14-25 (cf. GS 10, 13).

At the same time, we recognize and affirm the excellence of human freedom. Since our nature is wounded but not destroyed, freedom is still a characteristic of an authentically human act (Catechism, no. 1745). We are able to choose that which is truly good.

An understanding of our redeemed, yet wounded, nature is the necessary starting point for communicating sexual morality in our Catholic schools (cf. TMHS 122-23). Although Catholic educators may frequently draw upon the insights of non-Catholic and even secular educators, we must turn to Christ and His Church for the fullness of truth when it comes to the human person and the human condition.

In particular, two worldviews foreign to Catholic teaching continue to surface in many sex education circles. (For a broader discussion representative of these two philosophies, see VS 32-33.)

One view (the "it's only natural" school) posits the goal of sex education as "helping young people to become comfortable with their sexuality." This approach necessarily fails because it presents sex in a narrow and incomplete way by focusing only

---

[3] Private correspondence dated February 12, 1990.

on the natural or biological aspects, while ignoring the super-natural dimension as designed by God.

Another view, more prevalent in public education, is that promiscuity cannot be avoided, so we need to "cut our losses" by making sure nonmarital sex is at least "safe" and infertile. Contraception (and, as a "backup," abortion) is the answer.

These false worldviews undermine the virtues of self-control and generosity that are necessary to lead a chaste life. They also fail to recognize that the only realistic and practical solution to unwanted pregnancy and disease is chastity. We must dispel the "safe-sex" myth.

A successful chastity program must find the balance between recognizing the universal tendency to become unchaste and affirming a teen's ability, with God's grace, to choose to be chaste. The young person must not only learn to fight tempta-tion, but also to nurture a life of prayer that will allow him or her to receive the grace of purity (cf. 1 Cor. 6:19-20).

The Goal: Education in Chastity

From the preceding discussion of the effects of original sin, it should be clear that the principal requirement for chastity is divine grace, not mere information. Any presentation on the moral formation of youth must have a pervading empha-sis on prayer, and especially the Sacraments of Reconciliation and the Eucharist. If we want to be faithful to God and resist temptations, we must grow in self-knowledge and discipline, remain obedient to God's commandments, develop the moral virtues, and persevere in prayer (Catechism, no. 2340).

Chastity is a gift of grace, the fruit of spiritual effort. As Catholics we must teach our youth that they need to be wise and humble concerning their sexuality, and to take advantage of all available spiritual helps, including a vibrant devotion to Mary, Virgin Most Chaste (cf. Catechism, no. 971). The goal of chastity education is to enable the child to embrace his or her vocation in life lovingly and generously, and thereby grow in holiness.

In the Rite of Marriage, the couple is asked: "Will you accept children lovingly from God, and bring them up according to the law of Christ and His Church?" The second half of this question simply means that parents must commit themselves to help their children claim their heavenly inheritance. What is needed, then, is not a separate-track sex education course, but rather a strengthening of the religion course that will cover in a thoroughly Catholic way, and in a manner always appropriate to the age of the child, the Sixth and Ninth Commandments. Such an approach would indeed be education in chastity, providing the strongest doctrinal context while avoiding presentations that lose sight of this important goal (cf. Catechism, nos. 2337-56, 2514-33).

Aside from the merits of a particular sex education program, it seems odd to many parents that their children, with amazing technical accuracy, can identify male and female body parts and diverse modes of contraception, yet know precious little of Jesus Christ and especially His moral teachings.

Here, of course, we must again acknowledge the parents' primary responsibility for the child's religious and moral formation, and widespread deficiencies of such formation at home are at the root of the current problems with "sex education." *Calling parents to their proper duty must be a primary concern of Catholic educators. Strong families are the most effective means of fostering a living faith in the next generation. Such a faith will lead not only to chastity, but to the goal of chastity education: holiness.*

Graphic Illustrations

There is a formidable, unbroken line of Church documents promulgated this century that rejects an overly biological approach to sex education. This approach turns the program, in the crudest sense, into a "how-to" course. At the risk of sounding old-fashioned, should it not be a "how to wait until marriage" course?

Illustrative of this magisterial concern are the following two quotes from Pope John Paul II:

> Purely "biological" knowledge of the functions of the body as an organism, connected with the masculinity and femininity of the human person, is capable of helping to discover the true nuptial meaning of the body, only if it is accompanied by an adequate spiritual maturity of the human person. Otherwise,

such knowledge can have quite the opposite effect; and this is confirmed by many experiences of our time.[4]

[T]he Church is firmly opposed to an often widespread form of imparting sex information dissociated from moral principles. This would merely be an introduction to the experience of pleasure and a stimulus leading to the loss of serenity—while still in the years of innocence—by opening the way to vice (FC 37).

As TMHS points out, not only should no material of an erotic nature be presented, but also "no one should ever be invited, let alone obliged, to act in any way that could objectively offend against modesty or which could . . . offend against his or her own delicacy or sense of privacy" (TMHS 127; cf. 133).

There are several additional concerns raised by parents throughout the country. Some courses do not account for the fact that children progress at different rates. A coeducational setting, as is increasingly the norm for our Catholic schools, is an inappropriate setting for the type of information that is being communicated. There is the further concern that many sex education programs violate the child's "latency" (i.e., prepuberty) period by presenting explicit, biological information prematurely.

These considerations—which are not meant to be exhaustive—should motivate us to reexamine the objectives of a sex education program to the extent it ventures beyond moral formation into biological and physiological issues. In this regard, the document *Educational Guidance in Human Love*, issued by the Congregation for Catholic Education in 1983, is particularly noteworthy:

Some school textbooks on sexuality, by reason of their naturalist character, are harmful to the child and the adolescent. Graphic and audio-visual materials are more harmful when they crudely present sexual realities for which the child is not prepared, and thus create traumatic impressions or raise an unhealthy curiosity which leads to evil. Let teachers think

---

[4] General Audience (April 28, 1981).

seriously of the grave harm that an irresponsible attitude in such delicate matters can cause in pupils (no. 76).

Many Catholic school teachers are sincere in their desire to promote chastity, but these programs inevitably have the opposite effect. This is because using such a program is like trying to put out a fire with a bucket of gasoline. From a merely practical standpoint, it is legitimate to ask why, during the past quarter century, the more graphic programs have been associated with increases in premarital sex, divorce, sexually transmitted disease, contraceptive use, abortion, etc., instead of diminishing these problems.

Sex Is Sacred

There is a false presumption held by some and perpetuated by others that classical Catholic teaching holds that sex is bad or evil. In contrast, there is a modern view that regards sex as good and healthy. In reality, Catholic teaching has always considered sex as not merely good but *sacred*, which is why it is reserved for a committed marital covenant (Catechism, nos. 2360-63) that images the relationship between Christ and the Church (Eph. 5:32). Just as it would be a sacrilege to take the Eucharist outside and eat It with a Coke, so too taking sex outside of marriage is sacrilegious and results in gravely sinful activity (Catechism, nos. 2380-2400; cf. VS 79 *et seq.*).

Teaching the Teacher

Parents, in sending their children to Catholic schools, have the right to insist that the teachers, particularly those involved in moral formation, are "outstanding for their correct doctrine and integrity of life" (canon 803 §2; cf. GE 8). Unfortunately, that has not been the recent experience of many faithful, concerned parents. Conversely, many faithful religious educators have not had the support of parents who are likewise committed to sound Catholic doctrine.

Surveys report that at least fifty percent of American Catholics reject some aspect of the Church's teaching on sexual morality. Even assuming the average Catholic school teacher is twice as likely to be faithful, that still leaves one fourth of all

Catholic school teachers with a serious problem when it comes to education in chastity. Why would a youth, driven by so many different voices and impulses, look to the Church as the one sure guide to faith and morals when the teacher is not convinced of that fact?

This brings us back to the central role of the parents. Even the best of programs are limited. The most critical element of a child's spiritual formation, including chastity education, takes place at home, in the "domestic Church." This is the place where the child not only receives instruction, but experiences firsthand how Christian love manifests itself in the family. Therefore, the primary focus must be on the formation and education of parents. That way, parents are placed in a positive, active role in their children's education, and are not marginalized or left with the role of "critic" or "censor" of a school program. This empowerment of parents is not only best for their children, but also will frequently lead to a deepening of their own chaste commitment to Jesus Christ and His Church.

Questions for Reflection
or Group Discussion

1. Why is the issue of "sex education" or "chastity education" in schools such an important issue today? Why does the issue seem to cause such sharp differences of opinion? What can I do to foster greater understanding of the Church's teachings concerning chastity education?

2. (For parents) How do I, through word and example, foster the virtue of chastity in my children? What are my family's rules on dating or courtship? On entertainment choices? On modesty?

3. There are, unfortunately, "chastity" programs used in some Catholic schools that do not seem to meet the criteria set forth by the Church in TMHS. Appendix II provides a protocol for effectively addressing such issues. As a parent, what options do I have when my children are required to attend such programs? How can I seek redress without allowing my frustrations to make the situation worse?

Chapter 18

WHERE IN THE BIBLE . . . ?
The Catholic Response to *Sola Scriptura*

What does sola scriptura *mean? What is the Catholic response to this doctrine?*

Sola scriptura is the Protestant doctrine that Scripture alone is "the primary and absolute source of authority, the final court of appeal for all doctrine and practice [faith and morals]," and that "the Bible—nothing more, nothing less, and nothing else—is all that is necessary for faith and practice."[1]

The Second Vatican Council summarizes the Catholic response to *sola scriptura*, teaching that the Church

> does not derive her certainty about all revealed truths from the holy Scriptures alone. Both Scripture and Tradition must be accepted and honored with equal sentiments of devotion and reverence (Catechism, no. 82, quoting DV 9; see generally Catechism, nos. 74-87).

Many Catholics find themselves confronted with questions from Protestant friends about this or that belief or practice of the Church. Why do you baptize babies? Why do you pray for the dead? Why do you have statues? Why do you adore the Eucharist? Where does the Bible use the word "purgatory"? And what about all those unbiblical Marian beliefs?

If the hapless Catholic mumbles something about "Tradition" under his breath to explain his belief and practice, the Protestant has a ready reply, which may go something like this:

---

[1] Norman L. Geisler and Ralph E. MacKenzie, *Roman Catholics and Evangelicals: Agreements and Differences* (Grand Rapids, MI: Baker Book House Co., 1995), 178.

Jesus condemned the traditions of men (Mt. 15:3). Likewise, the apostles condemn adopting "philosophy and empty deceit, . . . according to the elemental spirits of the universe, and not according to Christ" (Col. 2:8). Instead of tradition, the true Christian should base his faith on the Bible alone, since it is totally and completely sufficient "for teaching, for reproof, for correction, and for training in righteousness, that the man of God may be complete, equipped for every good work" (2 Tim. 3:16-17). If "the Bible—nothing more, nothing less, and nothing else"—does not seem to you to clearly and unambiguously teach these Catholic doctrines, then you should not believe them.

Such arguments may seem very convincing. Nevertheless, upon closer inspection, they are found to be deeply flawed.

Sola Scriptura Is Unbiblical

If "the Bible and nothing else" is all that is necessary for faith and practice, then the Bible ought to make this doctrine clear, or at least imply this teaching at some point. The facts are otherwise: Scripture neither says nor implies that it alone is all that is necessary for faith and practice. Citations of Scripture's "proving" *sola scriptura* read into Scripture an intention that is not there. Thus, many arguments for *sola scriptura* will quote something like Deuteronomy 4:2—"You shall not add to the word which I command you, nor take from it"—to claim that Scripture alone is sufficient and that anything outside of what is written in Scripture cannot be God's Word or revelation. Such arguments neglect to note however that, logically applied, this claim means that the biblical books written *after* Deuteronomy are *also* "additions" to God's revelation.

In fact, what this and similar texts warn against is the addition of *human* wisdom to the Word of God. Scripture does *not* claim that God can only hand down revelation in written form. If God chose to reveal Himself further after the writing of Deuteronomy, and He did, or chooses to reveal Himself through some means other than writing, and He did— notably in the Incarnation of Jesus Christ—then the prohibition of Deuteronomy 4:2 does not apply.

Others will cite 2 Timothy 3:16 to claim that Scripture is a totally sufficient source of revelation. Here again, this neglects the question immediately raised by such a verse: Granting that all Scripture is "God-breathed," *how do we know which books are inspired Scripture and which books are not?* At the time 2 Timothy was composed, not all the New Testament books had even been written. By the time all the books of the New Testament were written, they were being circulated along with numerous other books and epistles of varying quality, all of which vied for the attention of the early Christians. If the "sufficiency" of Scripture of which Paul speaks is a *total* sufficiency, Scripture should somehow be able to answer the question, "How can we tell which books are inspired Scripture and which aren't?" But, in fact, Scripture does not do this, a fact attested by the different collections of "recognized" scriptural books which existed in the different early Christian Church communities. Similarly, even today different Christians have different canons or collections of Scripture.[2]

The "sufficiency of Scripture" of which Paul speaks is not, in fact, "formal" or total sufficiency. On the contrary, Scripture assumes that the written portion of apostolic Tradition is only "materially" sufficient revelation, and that the Church will rely on two additional authoritative sources to fully discern God's revelation: Sacred Tradition and the Magisterium or teaching office of the Church.

The difference between formal and material sufficiency is the difference between having a brick house and having a big enough pile of bricks to build a house. Drawing on this analogy, Christ the Master Builder uses the mortar of Tradition and the trowel of the Magisterium to build His brick house of revelation from a mere pile of bricks (cf. Mt. 16:18, Eph. 2:19-22; 1 Tim. 3:15). It is these three elements together—written Tradition (that is, Scripture), unwritten Tradition, and the Magisterium—that hand down the fullness of Revelation, who is Jesus Christ.

---

[2] Cf. "The Complete Bible: Why Catholics Have Seven More Books," available from Catholics United for the Faith, 827 N. Fourth St., Steubenville, OH 43952, (800) MY-FAITH, www.cuf.org.

166 THE CATHOLIC RESPONSE TO *SOLA SCRIPTURA*

This is the biblical witness as well. When the circumcision crisis arose around 40 A.D., there was, on a *sola scriptura* basis, an enormous amount of biblical precedent for the idea that Gentiles who wished to become Christians must be circumcised. After all,

1. everybody from the time of Abraham, including Our Lord and His apostles, had received circumcision, as God Himself had commanded (Gen. 17);
2. this requirement had always included Gentile converts to the Covenant People, as God Himself had also commanded (Ex. 12:48); and
3. Our Lord had never clearly abolished this requirement but had rather insisted that "till heaven and earth pass away, not an iota, not a dot, will pass from the law until all is accomplished" (Mt. 5:18).

Nonetheless, the Church concluded that circumcision was unnecessary for Gentiles to become Christians. How? By the clear recognition that the full teaching of Christ is obtained, not merely by reliance on the "Bible and nothing else," but by reading the Bible in the context of her Sacred Tradition, which is the common life, common teaching, and common worship of the apostolic Church (cf. Acts 2:42).

What the Church did was hold a council—the Council of Jerusalem (Acts 15)—so that the Magisterium of the Church, i.e., the apostles, their successors, and other Christian leaders, could examine not only Scripture but the full apostolic Tradition of the Church, both written and unwritten, and render an authoritative decision. At the Council, the Church sifted the *whole* of the apostolic message—not just the written part—and eventually concluded that, despite what Scripture alone *appeared* to say, the reality was that the New Covenant of Christ did not require circumcision for Gentile converts.

In fact, Scripture is treated by the Council of Jerusalem exactly as the Catholic Church still treats it today: as the written portion, not the totality, of God's revelation. Revelation is not a one-legged stool of Scripture alone, but a three-legged stool of written Tradition, unwritten Tradition and the Magisterium. This is why Saint Paul tells the Thessalonians to "hold to the traditions which you were taught by us, either by word of mouth or by letter" (2 Thess. 2:15). These are the first two legs of the stool. The Council of Jerusalem also illustrates why Paul appointed bishops, among them Timothy and Titus, to "guard the truth that has been entrusted to you by the Holy Spirit who dwells within us" (2 Tim. 1:14), for they constitute the essential third leg. Taken together, this three-legged stool gives us a sure basis for discerning authentic apostolic teaching. "Tradition" *per se* is not condemned by either Jesus or the apostles. Rather, it is only the "traditions of men" they condemned.

Who's to Judge?

If we reject this basic Catholic understanding of revelation, we immediately encounter enormous difficulties. Adherents of *sola scriptura* assert that Scripture alone is "perspicuous" or clear about the important things that God desires us to know for our salvation, and that that those passages which are less clear can be understood in light of passages which are more clear.

However, in practice this is plainly not so. Is the Eucharist the body and blood of Christ or is it a symbol? Swiss reformer Ulrich Zwingli believed that John 6:63—"It is the spirit that gives life, the flesh is of no avail"—"clearly" showed that Jesus was speaking symbolically of the Eucharist and that the "less clear" passages, such as Jesus' declaration, "This is my body" (Lk. 22:19) must be interpreted in light of John 6:63. Zwingli's conclusion: The Eucharist is just a symbol. Martin Luther, on the other hand, regarded "This is my body" as the clear passage and interpreted John 6:63 in light of it. Not surprisingly, Luther and Zwingli were bitter opponents and split over this issue.

In the same way, the foundational sacrament of the Christian life—Baptism—is open to wildly divergent beliefs and practices when left to the mercies of *sola scriptura*. Is Baptism for repentant adults only or for infants as well? Does it effect regeneration or is it only a symbol? Is it to be done in the name of the Blessed Trinity or in the name of Jesus only? All of these questions and many more have been "clearly" answered in one way by one group of *sola scriptura* adherents . . . and then just as "clearly" answered the opposite way by other groups of *sola scriptura* adherents. Scripture alone is not always clear, so various groups and individuals, based on their respective opinions, in practice take on the role of the divinely ordained Magisterium.

Inconsistent Application

Sola scriptura is often asserted to argue against aspects of Catholic Tradition unpalatable to a particular Protestant theology, and there are many of these. Thus, for instance, it is argued by most Evangelicals that the Real Presence in the Eucharist is weakly attested to by Scripture. It is argued that John 6 and the words "This is my body" can be interpreted several ways. And since "the Bible and nothing else" is all that is necessary for faith and practice, the ambiguity of Scripture alone on this point means the Catholic Church has no right to "add their Tradition to Scripture" and derive a dogmatic belief in the Real Presence. The same logic is applied again and again to various displeasing features of Catholic teaching, ranging from purgatory, to the office of Peter, to prayers for the dead.

Regarding "fundamental Christian doctrines," however, Evangelicals unconsciously function exactly like Catholics and read their Bibles in light of Sacred Tradition, which has percolated down to them from pre-Reformation Catholic Tradition. Thus, Evangelicals do not declare monogamy to be optional, even though Scripture alone is far *more* ambiguous about monogamy vs. polygamy than it is about purgatory or the Real Presence—a fact recognized by Martin Luther and his colleague Philip Melancthon.[3]

Likewise, belief in the sanctity of human life at conception is also very ambiguous on the basis of Scripture alone, as is the doctrine of the Trinity and, a teaching at the core of Evangelical "Bible only" belief, that public revelation closed with the death

---

[3] Martin Luther, *De Wette*, II, 459: "I confess that I cannot forbid a person to marry several wives, for it does not contradict the Scripture. If a man wishes to marry more than one wife, he should be asked whether he is satisfied in his conscience that he may do so in accordance with the Word of God. In such a case, the civil authority has nothing to do in such a matter."

of the apostles. Yet Evangelicals typically treat these doctrines with the same certainty that the Catholic Church treats the Real Presence. The reason for this is straightforward: Evangelicalism has unconsciously retained *part* of Sacred Tradition in such instances and reads Scripture in light of it, whereas the Catholic Church has retained the *fullness* of that same Tradition.

God's Word to Us

Sola scriptura is, ironically, a human tradition not found in Scripture, and it is a huge source of theological chaos and a doctrine not fully lived even by its adherents. Scripture is the written portion of the Church's Sacred Tradition. It cannot be separated from the whole of that Tradition and from the Catholic Church's magisterial authority without distorting the very message God intends us to discover in it.

Christians who look to the Bible as the sole rule of faith recognize the inherent power of the Scriptures. God's Word is truly "living and active" (Heb. 4:12), capable of changing the lives of those who have ears to hear (cf. Mt 11:15). In charitable discourse with "Bible Christians," "the sacred Word is a precious instrument in the mighty hand of God for attaining to that unity which the Savior holds out to all men" (UR 21).

May all Christians, in imitation of the Blessed Virgin Mary and all the saints, listen attentively to God's Word, ponder it in our hearts, apply it to our daily lives, and so strive for greater unity in the heart of Christ's Church (cf. Lk. 2:19; 11:28).

_____*SideBar*_____

Biblical Teaching on the Bible

- The first Christians "were persevering in the doctrine of the apostles" (Acts 2:42; cf. 2 Tim. 1:14) long before the New Testament was written—and centuries before the New Testament canon was settled.

- The Bible affirms that Christian teaching is "preached" (1 Pet. 1:25), that the apostles' successors were to teach what they have "heard" (2 Tim. 2:2), and that Christian teaching is passed on both "by word of mouth [and] by letter" (2 Thess. 2:15; cf. 1 Cor. 11:2).

- Not everything Christ did is recorded in Sacred Scripture (Jn. 21:25).

- New Testament authors availed themselves of Sacred Tradition. For example, Acts 20:35 quotes a saying of Jesus that is not recorded in the Gospels.

- Scripture needs an authoritative interpreter (Acts 8:30-31; 2 Pet. 1:20-21, 3:15-16).

- Christ left a Church with divine authority to teach in His name (Mt. 16:13-20, 18:18; Lk. 10:16). The Church will last until the end of time, and the Holy Spirit protects the Church's teaching from corruption (Mt. 16:18, 28:19-20; Jn. 14:16).

- The Church—and not the Bible alone—is the "pillar and bulwark of the truth" (1 Tim. 3:15).

- The Bible does not refer to Scripture as the exclusive source of the Word of God. Jesus Himself is the Word (Jn. 1:1, 14), and in 1 Thessalonians 2:13, Saint Paul's first epistle, he refers to "the Word of God which you heard from us." There Saint Paul is clearly referring to oral apostolic teaching: *Tradition.*

Questions for Reflection
or Group Discussion

1. Saint Jerome once wrote, "Ignorance of Scripture is ignorance of Christ." What does he mean? How can I deepen my knowledge and understanding of Sacred Scripture?

2. Can I demonstrate from the Bible that *sola scriptura* is not taught in Scripture. What passages would I use?

3. Read Catechism, nos. 80-87. How do I understand Sacred Tradition? What is the role of the Magisterium in preserving and proclaiming God's Word?

Chapter 19

HIS NAME IS JOHN
The Beloved Disciple and Author of the Fourth Gospel

Is the Apostle John the beloved disciple and author of the fourth Gospel?

Yes. The Church, which alone has been given the task of interpreting God's written and spoken Word, has consistently taught that Saint John was the beloved disciple and the author of the Gospel "According to John."

Some biblical scholars say that John the Apostle is neither the beloved disciple nor the author of the fourth Gospel. They even question whether we can accept the Gospels, particularly the Gospel of John, as genuinely historical accounts. For example, some question whether the author of the Gospel was really at the Cross during Christ's crucifixion (cf. Jn. 19:35; 21:21-24), or whether this was a later literary embellishment by the evangelist himself or the Christian faithful.

The Fourth Gospel:
Are We Even Dealing with History?

In his 1920 encyclical *Spiritus Paraclitus*, a document on biblical studies which commemorated the 1,500th anniversary of the death of Saint Jerome, Pope Benedict XV addressed those who deny the historicity of the Gospels:

> They refuse to allow that the things which Christ said or did have come down to us unchanged and entire through witnesses who carefully committed to writing what they themselves had seen or heard. They maintain—and particularly in their treatment of the *Fourth Gospel*—that much is due of course to the Evangelists—who, however, added much from their own imaginations; but much, too, is due to narratives

compiled by the faithful at other periods, the result, of course, being that the twin streams now flowing in the same channel cannot be distinguished from one another (no. 27, original emphasis).

In responding to these critics, Pope Benedict noted that both Saints Augustine and Jerome affirmed the historical reliability of the Gospels: "None can doubt but that what is written took place," wrote Saint Jerome (in *ibid.*). For his part, the Pope himself quotes John 19:35 approvingly: "He who saw it has borne witness, and his witness is true; and he knows that he tells the truth, that you also may believe" (SP 27). The evangelist writes this immediately following his account of the crucifixion of Christ, an account which noted that the "disciple whom he loved" was at the Cross with Jesus' mother Mary (Jn. 19:26).

The Gospel of John elsewhere provides details that indicate a historical, eyewitness account. For example, the author notes that the stone wine jars at the wedding at Cana were filled to the brim (Jn. 2:7); the loaves used in the miraculous multiplication near the Sea of Galilee were made of barley (Jn. 6:9); and the fragrance of the perfume Mary used to anoint Jesus' feet filled the house in which they were staying (Jn. 12:3).

In Search of the Beloved Disciple
The author of John provides key details in chapter 21 to help us narrow the field of candidates for the "beloved disciple." The evangelist identifies himself as the beloved disciple (Jn. 21:20-24). In this passage, he also notes that Peter is *not* the beloved disciple, and that the beloved disciple "had lain close to his breast at the [Last Supper] and had said, 'Lord, who is it that is going to betray you?'" (Jn. 21:20; cf. 13:23-25; 20:2). From this account, we know that the beloved disciple was at the Last Supper.

From the Gospels of Mark (14:17-26) and Matthew (26:20-30), we learn that only the twelve apostles were with Jesus at the Last Supper. Even Luke 22:14 notes that it was just "the apostles" who were present with Jesus for the Last Supper, as opposed to a larger gathering of disciples.

With the field narrowed to the apostles, we know we can immediately eliminate not only Peter but also Judas. We could also reasonably conclude that the beloved disciple would have a qualitatively different relationship with Jesus from most of the other disciples. In other words, we would expect closer collaboration between him and the Lord. In this light, we discover that three apostles—Peter, John, and John's brother James— spent more time with Christ than did the others. Jesus singles out this trio to accompany Him to the healing of Jairus' daughter (Mk. 5:22-24, 35-43), the Mount of Transfiguration (Mk. 9:2-10), and the Garden of Gethsemane on Holy Thursday evening (Mk. 14:32-33). In addition, in John 1:14, the Gospel author notes that "we have beheld his glory," a reference perhaps not just to having seen the resurrected Christ, but also to having witnessed His glorious Transfiguration, something only Peter, James, and John witnessed.

James or John?

Because Peter is distinguished from the beloved disciple, we therefore narrow the field to the "sons of thunder" (Mk. 3:17), James and John. Biblical scholars date the writing of John anywhere from the late 60s to the first decade of the second century. Any year in that time period would necessarily exclude James, whom Herod Agrippa killed (Acts 12:2) during his reign in the early 40s.

This leaves us with John the Apostle as the only plausible choice as the beloved disciple. The Bible does not indicate anyone else, and the early Church only proposed John as the Gospel author and thus the beloved disciple. Saint Irenaeus (d. 202), for example, in writing about the authors of the various Gospels, notes that after Luke wrote his Gospel, "John, the disciple of the Lord who reclined at His bosom, also published a Gospel, while he was residing at Ephesus in Asia."[1]

Finally, in May 1907, the Pontifical Biblical Commission (PBC) issued a declaration on the matter, affirming that

---

[1] Saint Irenaeus, *Against the Heresies*, 3, 1, 1; as quoted in William A. Jurgens, ed., *The Faith of the Early Fathers*, vol. 1 (Collegeville, MN: The Liturgical Press, 1970), 89.

prescinding from theological proof, it is demonstrated by such strong historical proof that John the Apostle and no other is to be recognized as the author of the fourth Gospel, that the reasons adduced by critics in opposition by no means weakens this tradition.[2]

It is important to note that the PBC still had magisterial status[3] at the time of its 1907 response. By affirming the beloved disciple's eyewitness authorship of the fourth Gospel (Jn. 19:35), Pope Benedict implicitly supports the PBC's 1907 affirmation of John as the beloved disciple and the author of the fourth Gospel.

Some biblical scholars still say that the beloved disciple could not be John because of the prophecy foretold in Zechariah 13:7: "Strike the shepherd, that the sheep may be scattered. . . ." Following the Last Supper, Jesus told His disciples that this prophecy would be fulfilled that same Holy Thursday evening:

You will all fall away because of me this night; for it is written, 'I will strike the shepherd, and the sheep of the flock will be scattered.' But after I am raised up, I will go before you to Galilee" (Mt. 26:31-32; cf. Mk. 14:27-28; Jn. 16:32).

Some scholars argue that if all the apostles had fallen away or abandoned Jesus to fulfill Zechariah 13:7 (Mt. 26:56), none of them could have been around to stand by Our Lord at the foot of His Cross. However, the disciples' scattering does not preclude the possibility that some of them could have come back later. Peter is later described as following Christ "at a distance" (Mk. 14:54). In addition, John 18:15 identifies another disciple

---

[2] As quoted in Henry Denziger, ed., *The Sources of Catholic Dogma* (St. Louis: B. Herder Book Co., 1957), trans. by Roy J. Deferrari, no. 2110.

[3] Until 1971, the PBC's documents had magisterial authority. In that year, however, Pope Paul VI removed its magisterial status. The PBC is currently only an advisory body that reports to the Congregation for the Doctrine of the Faith (CDF). The CDF maintains this magisterial status. See Pope Paul VI, *Motu Proprio* "Biblical Commission: New Regulatory Laws," June 27, 1971 (AAS 63-665), as cited in *Canon Law Digest*, vol. 7 (Chicago: Chicago Province of the Society of Jesus), 184-88.

near Christ after the scattering, one "known to the high priest," who "entered the court of the high priest along with Jesus, while Peter stood outside the door." This other disciple was likely the Apostle John.

In his *Ecclesiastical History*, the eminent early Church historian Eusebius noted that John came from a priestly family.[4] This is significant because the author of the fourth Gospel demonstrates an extensive knowledge of Jewish liturgy and Jerusalem, the city in which Jewish liturgy (i.e., the sacrificial aspects) took place. Finally, as we have learned from previous analysis of the Gospels, the beloved disciple was not only at the Cross but also had to be one of the twelve apostles.

Testimony of the Church

When the Bible itself or its particular books and passages are called into question, we turn to the Catholic Church that Jesus Christ founded (Mt. 16:18). He commissioned the Church to teach everything that Christ had commanded (Mt. 28:20), and established the Church as the pillar and foundation of truth (1 Tim. 3:15). Only the teaching office of the Catholic Church—the Pope and the bishops in union with him—have been given authority to authentically interpret the Word of God, whether written down in Scripture or handed down in the form of Tradition (Catechism, no. 85). In submitting to the Church, we demonstrate faithfulness to Christ (cf. Lk. 10:16), who promised to be with His Church until the end of time (Mt. 28:20; cf. Jn. 16:13).

The Church has always identified the Apostle John as the author of the fourth Gospel and the beloved disciple, and this is richly reflected in the Church's liturgy. The universal Church celebrates the Feast of Saint John, Apostle and *Evangelist*, on December 27. The readings and antiphons unmistakably reflect the belief of the Church concerning these issues. For example, one of the antiphons for morning prayer on this feast day states: "John, the apostle and evangelist, a virgin chosen by the Lord, was loved by the Lord above the others."

---

[4] Eusebius, *The History of the Church*, bk. 3, 31, 3 (New York: Penguin Books, 1965), trans. by G.A. Williamson.

The Church clearly teaches that the Gospels are historically true (DV 19) and that the beloved disciple was really at the foot of the Cross during Christ's crucifixion. We should not be surprised that such a beloved disciple would be with Christ in His time of greatest trial. Such is the nature of true love.

Questions for Reflection
or Group Discussion

1. What proof is there that the Apostle John is the "beloved disciple" and the author of the fourth Gospel? How would I explain the authorship of the fourth Gospel to someone who rejects the authority of the Church?

2. Does the questioning of John's authorship by some Catholic scholars build the Catholic faith? Why is it important to affirm the Church's position on this matter?

3. Why did Saint John refer to himself as the "beloved disciple"? What does this say about his relationship with Christ?

Chapter 20

RELATIVE OBSCURITY
The "Brothers and Sisters" of Jesus

How can the Catholic Church teach that Mary was a virgin after the birth of Christ when there are references in Scripture to the "brothers and sisters" of Jesus?

There are portions of Scripture that refer to the "brothers and sisters" of Jesus Christ. These passages seem to contradict the Church's teaching that Mary remained a virgin after the birth of Christ. However, if we carefully examine these passages in context, it becomes clear that these "brothers and sisters" are *not* other biological children of the Blessed Mother. Further, in light of both Scripture and Tradition, we know that Jesus had brothers and sisters in the broader sense of the words, that is, His cousins.[1]

When looking for biblical "evidence" against Mary's Perpetual Virginity, some Christians typically cite passages referring to the "brothers and sisters" of Jesus in Matthew 13:55-56 and Mark 6:3 (see also Mk. 3:31; Lk. 8:20; Jn. 2:1; 7:3-5; Acts 1:14; Gal. 1:19; 1 Cor. 9:5). Although the Greek word *adelphos* is used in these passages and literally translates as "brother" (also *adelphē*, "sister"), resolving this issue is not as simple as it seems on the surface.

---

[1] Catholics believe that some passages of Scripture *imply* Mary's Perpetual Virginity, but only Sacred Tradition teaches it *explicitly*. Nevertheless, it absolutely *does not contradict* Scripture. For more information on Mary's Perpetual Virginity, see the chapter entitled "Always a Virgin" in Hahn and Suprenant, eds., *Catholic for a Reason II: Scripture and the Mystery of the Mother of God* (Steubenville, OH: Emmaus Road Publishing, 1999), available fall 1999.

Dynamic Translation

To understand Sacred Scripture and the intended meaning of words, we must understand the idioms used at that time and how translators have rendered the biblical passages into our modern language. Every language uses idioms. An idiom is an expression of words that does not mean what it literally says. The intended meaning is different, but people of the same culture understand the intended meaning because of the context of the statement and their knowledge of the language. For example, "quit pulling my leg" usually means "stop telling untrue stories." If this idiom were translated into another language, the translator would probably not use a literal translation. If he did, the wrong impression would be given. Instead, he would use the words of his language that best mean the same thing the idiom intended. This is called a *dynamic* translation. However, if the people using the translation understood the idiom, he would probably translate it *literally* so his audience could appreciate the original statement.

Hebrew, which is the original language of the Old Testament, and Aramaic, which is the language spoken by the Jews of Israel in Jesus' day, do not have a word for cousin, nephew, or various other kinsmen. To say "cousin" in Hebrew or Aramaic, one must either say "son of my father's brother" or, the more common choice, "brother" (Heb. *ach*). Your Bible in English will probably tell you in Genesis 14:14 that Lot is Abraham's "nephew" or "kinsman." There is no question that Lot is the son of Abraham's brother (Gen. 12:5) and thus his nephew. But the typical translation of Genesis 14:14, as "nephew" or "kinsman," is a *dynamic* one. The *literal* translation of Genesis 14:14 actually says that Lot is Abraham's brother. Why?

When Jews translated the Old Testament into Greek—the version called the "Septuagint" or "LXX"—they had two options. They could translate Genesis 14:14 dynamically, because Greek has a word that means "nephew." On the other hand, they could translate it literally as "brother," following the Hebrew expression or idiom. Because they were Jews who understood the Hebrew idiom, they chose the Greek word *adelphos* (brother) as a translation of *ach* (brother, relative). This is a consistent practice in the Old Testament.[2] In contrast, the English translators use a dynamic translation and call Lot Abraham's nephew.

It's All Greek to Me

When the New Testament authors wrote in Greek, they too were faced with a choice. Jesus, His family, and His disciples spoke Aramaic. The audience of these authors generally used the Septuagint version of Sacred Scripture and were accustomed to the Aramaic idiom. The authors could follow the example of the Septuagint[3] and the Aramaic idiom, calling cousins and other kinsmen "brothers," or they could use a dynamic translation, such as the Greek word *anepsios* (cousin). They chose to follow the Aramaic idiom, which was the most natural choice given their sources, and thus used the word *adelphos* (or the plural, *adelphoi*) for cousins and kinsmen. In contrast to the dynamic translations of the Old Testament, English translations often translate the New Testament literally and use the word "brother."

How do we know that the New Testament writers followed the Aramaic idiom? There are two reasons. First, the Greek word for cousin is never used in the New Testament. Second, we know that certain people were not "brothers" or "sisters" even though the literal translation implies it. For example, Matthew 27:56 speaks of Mary the mother of James and Joseph. Matthew 27:61 and 28:1 refer to her as "the other Mary." Mary the mother of Jesus is never identified as "the other Mary." John 19:25 identifies "the other Mary" as the wife of Clopas, who is called the *adelphē* (sister) of Jesus' mother Mary (Jn. 19:25). Matthew and John both list a Mary other than the mother of Jesus and Mary Magdalene. This is the same Mary in both Gospels, but we learn different things about her from the two Gospel writers. John tells us that she is Mary, the wife of

---

[2] Consider also 1 Chronicles 23:22, which said Kish died having no sons, only daughters. These daughters then married their kinsmen, that is, their cousins or relatives, who themselves are described as the "sons of Kish."

[3] The apostles preferred to use the Septuagint version of Sacred Scripture. The New Testament is heavily dependent on the Septuagint's writing style and Greek usage. For more information on the Septuagint, see CUF's FAITH FACT on the canon of Scripture.

Clopas. Matthew tells us she is the mother of James and Joseph. Were Mary the wife of Clopas and Jesus' mother actually sisters as the Gospel of John states? It is very unlikely that two children of the same parents would be given the *same* name, so *adelphē* seems to be used by the New Testament authors in a broader sense here (cousin, kinswoman).

Matthew, Mark, and John, however, provide us with clearer evidence refuting the scriptural arguments that Mary had other children besides Jesus. John notes that Mary the wife of Clopas was present at Jesus' crucifixion (19:25). In Matthew and Mark's account of the crucifixion, this same Mary is also described as the mother of James and Joseph (Mt. 27:56; Mk. 15:40). But James and Joseph are *also* described as the "brothers" (*adelphoi*) of Jesus in Matthew 13:55 and Mark 6:3. How can this be? If Mary the wife of Clopas is the sister (cousin) of Mary the mother of Jesus and the mother of James and Joseph, then clearly James and Joseph are not Jesus' biological brothers. Rather, they are His cousins. In other words, in Matthew 13:55 *adelphoi* is being used in the Aramaic idiom ("cousins") rather than its literal Greek meaning ("brothers"). In addition, because James and Joseph are not distinguished from Jesus' other brothers and sisters in Matthew 13 and Mark 6, we can logically conclude that these other brothers and sisters are Jesus' cousins too.

There is no linguistic reason to believe that this is not true of all Jesus' "brothers and sisters." Because *adelphoi* does not always refer to literal brothers in New Testament Greek usage, Jesus' "brothers and sisters" cannot form the basis of a conclusive argument against Mary's Perpetual Virginity.

Relative Clauses

Similar arguments, based on the meaning of the words "until" and "before" and "first-born,"[4] do not refute Mary's Perpetual Virginity either. They are based on false linguistic

---

[4] The best refutation of the "before" and "until" arguments against Mary's Perpetual Virginity is found in Saint Jerome's *On the Perpetual Virginity of the Blessed Mary: Against Helvidius.* (This work is available in various collections of the writings of the

assumptions. For example, passages often cited to deny Mary's remaining a virgin after Jesus' birth include Matthew 1:18, which reads, "before they came together she was found to be with child of the Holy Spirit. . . ." This is often cited along with Matthew 1:25, which says that Joseph "knew her not until she had borne a son; and he called his name Jesus." The argument contends that the "before" and "until" clauses here imply that Mary and Joseph had marital relations following the birth of Christ. Yet, if understood properly, this is not necessarily the case.

In the Bible's languages, as in the English language prior to modern times, clauses which begin with "before" or "until" ("till") do not necessarily imply that after the completion of an action there followed a reversal of the situation described. In other words, to say "x did not happen until y" only meant that "x" did not happen up to a certain point in time (i.e., "y"); it did *not necessarily* mean that "x" *did* happen after "y." A clear example can be found in Paul's words to Timothy, "Till I come, attend to the public reading of Scripture, to preaching, to teaching. . ." (1 Tim. 4:13). Obviously, Paul did not mean to suggest that Timothy should give up these activities after his arrival. Another such use of the "until" clause is found in Psalm 123:2, which reads, "Behold, as the eyes of servants look to the hand of their master, as the eyes of a maid to the hand of her mistress, so our eyes look to the Lord our God, *till* he have mercy upon us." Obviously, the psalmist does not mean that we should take our eyes off the Lord *after* He has mercy on us![5]

Church Fathers.) Jerome, the patron saint of Scripture scholars, translated the Bible into Latin from Hebrew and Greek. The claim that Jesus had literal brothers and sisters was completely "novel" (his own word) in Jerome's time, and he refutes this flawed linguistic argument thoroughly.

[5] Other examples include Deuteronomy 34:5-6, 2 Samuel 6:23, Isaiah 46:4, Matthew 28:20, Romans 8:22, 1 Corinthians 15:25, Ephesians 4:13, 1 Timothy 6:14, and Revelation 2:25-26. Some modern translations use "to" or "till" instead of "until," but the sense is the same. Check your Bible and see. "Until" cannot be used as an argument against Mary's continued virginity. In addition, "He had not known her when she bore a son" (Knox translation), is a linguistically acceptable translation of Matthew 1:25, so this verse cannot be used to refute Mary's Perpetual Virginity.

The "before" clause, we know from experience, can be used in much the same way. A biblical example may be found in John 4:49, "Come down before my child dies." From the context of the passage, we know that the child did not die— he was healed.

First and Last

Opponents of Mary's Perpetual Virginity also cite the passage that identifies Jesus as her "first-born" (Lk. 2:7). They argue that Jesus could not be called Mary's "first-born" unless she and Joseph had more children after His birth. While this argument may seem persuasive in our present culture, we must understand its usage in the light of the Middle Eastern culture of the time. For the Jews of Jesus' time and their neighbors, "first-born" was always used to refer to the first male child of a marriage, regardless of whether other children were subsequently born to the couple. It was an important legal and religious term meaning that there were no prior male children.

To understand this better, look at Exodus 13. The Lord said to Moses that Israel should "set apart to the Lord all that first opens the womb" (Ex. 13:12). This included "first-born" male humans: "Every first-born of man among your sons you shall redeem" (Ex. 13:13b; cf. Num. 3:12; Lk. 2:22-23). Further evidence is found in Exodus 12, when the first-born of Egypt die. Verse 12:30 says, "[T]here was not [an Egyptian] house where one was not dead." This would include the houses of young couples who only had one son.[6] That Jesus was Mary and Joseph's "first-born" cannot refute Mary's Perpetual Virginity.

Ark of the Covenant

In the words of noted Protestant theologian John de Satgé, "There is *certainly nothing in the Scriptures* to invalidate the con-

---

[6] Likewise, an ancient Egyptian funerary inscription tells of a woman who died during the birth of her "first-born," though it would be impossible for her to have children after that. See Karl Keating, *Catholicism and Fundamentalism* (San Francisco: Ignatius Press, 1988), 286.

clusion of the [ancient] Church . . . that Mary was a virgin all her life."[7] On the contrary, Mary's Perpetual Virginity is implied in the Bible.[8] For example, when Gabriel tells Mary (a betrothed woman) that she will conceive (a future event), Mary responds, "*How* can this be? I do not know man" (Lk. 1:34). The phrase "know man" is a Hebrew idiom for sexual intercourse (cf. Gen. 4:1), so Mary clearly knows where babies come from. "How can this be?" is an unusual thing for a betrothed woman to say. In the words of Saint Augustine:

> Because she had made a vow of virginity and her husband did not have to be the thief of her modesty instead of its guardian (and yet her husband was not its guardian, since it was God who guarded it; her husband was only the witness of her virginal chastity, so that her pregnancy would not be considered the result of adultery), when the angel brought her the news, she said: "How can this be, since I do not know man?" (Lk 1:34). Had she intended to know man, she would not have been amazed. Her amazement is a sign of the vow.[9]

Indeed, Mary's question, "How can this be?" only makes sense if Mary had previously decided to remain a virgin after her marriage. Gabriel's answer, of course, is that the conception of Jesus will be miraculous, that is, by the power of the Holy Spirit (Lk. 1:35).

Further, it is interesting to note that the Bible clearly refers to Mary as Jesus' mother, but does not ever directly mention her as someone else's mother, for example, as the "mother of Jesus and Joseph" or "with her was James, her son." The most obvious reason for this, given the other evidence, is that she was *not* the mother of Jesus' "brothers and sisters."

---

[7] As quoted in Fr. Mateo, *Refuting the Attack on Mary* (San Diego: Catholic Answers, 1993), 4 (emphasis added).
[8] This probably explains why the major Protestant reformers (e.g., Luther, Calvin, and Zwingli) continued to believe in Mary's Perpetual Virginity even after they denied the authority of the Church.
[9] St. Augustine of Hippo, Sermo 225, 2, as quoted in Luigi Gambero, S.M., *Mary and the Fathers of the Church* (San Francisco: Ignatius Press, 1999), 221.

Finally, the ark of the covenant in the Old Testament has been traditionally viewed by Christians as a type of Mary. Like the ark which carried the Old Covenant (represented by the tablets of the Law), Mary carried in her womb Jesus the New Covenant. This is why some biblical scholars argue that the mother of the Messiah (Mary) is mentioned immediately after the ark of the covenant in the Book of Revelation (11:19-12:1, 5, 17). The old ark and Mary appear to John at the same time because Mary is the ark of the New Covenant. What was one of the special characteristics of the ark of the Old Covenant? No one could touch it directly and live, because of its holiness; it was blessed by the Lord's presence (2 Sam. 6:6-15).

Mary, likewise, was "full of grace" (Lk. 1:28)[10] and carried the Lord in her womb, and it is unlikely that a pious man (like Joseph) would want to "touch" someone set apart for the Lord. The Church Fathers, who believed the Church's Sacred Tradition of Mary's Perpetual Virginity, also believed that this was a reasonable and very scriptural conclusion.

Questions for Reflection or Group Discussion

1. How do I defend the Church's constant teaching on Mary's Perpetual Virginity when confronted with the objection that the Bible mentions Jesus' "brothers"?

2. Does the Bible *prove* Mary's Perpetual Virginity? Does it disprove it? How can I confidently interpret passages that relate to Jesus' "brothers"?

3. Why is Mary's Perpetual Virginity important? How does it affect my life?

---

[10] The Greek word *kecharitōménē* is best translated "full of grace" or "perfected in grace," not merely "favored."

THE FIRST MARIAN DOGMA
Mary, Mother of God

What is the Church's teaching concerning Mary's divine maternity?

The first and foremost revealed truth about our Blessed Mother, from which all her other roles and honors flow, is that she is the Mother of God.

Catechism, no. 509 summarizes the teaching as follows: "Mary is truly 'Mother of God' since she is the mother of the eternal Son of God made man, who is God himself." The title "Mother of God" points to the sublime truth of the Incarnation, that Jesus Christ is true God and true man.

The Church's teaching concerning Mary's divine maternity is deeply rooted in Scripture and Tradition, and was dogmatically defined at the Council of Ephesus in 431. The Church celebrates this mystery of our Catholic faith on January 1.

For many Catholics, Mary's "divine maternity"—in other words, her status as the "Mother of God"—is almost second nature. One of our oldest and most recited prayers, the Hail Mary, explicitly invokes "Holy Mary, Mother of God." We typically call Mary our "Blessed Mother," which points to our participation in the divine life as adopted children of God (cf. Rom. 8:15-17; Gal. 4:4-7; Rev. 12:17). We could not call her *our* Blessed Mother unless she was first and foremost *His* Blessed Mother.

Since the fifth century, Mary's title as "Mother of God" has been firmly established, and is easily the least controversial of the Christian doctrines concerning Mary. This teaching thus is a good starting point for ecumenical discussion and, as will be shown below, preserves correct teaching concerning who Jesus Christ is.

As we prepare for the celebration of Jesus' 2,000th birthday, let us take a closer look at His mother, from whom "the Word became flesh" (Jn. 1:14).

The Logic of Scripture

The Bible nowhere uses the expression "Mother of God." But Mary is clearly identified as the "mother of Jesus" (cf. Mt. 2:13, 20; Lk. 1:31; 2:34; Acts 1:14) and mother of the Son of God (cf. Lk. 1:35; Gal. 4:4). Even before the birth of Jesus, Elizabeth proclaims that Mary is "the mother of my Lord" (Lk. 1:43; cf. Catechism, no. 495). Clearly, Mary is identified throughout the New Testament as the mother of Our Lord and Savior Jesus Christ.

Catechism, no. 481 summarizes the fundamental Christian belief that Jesus Christ is true God and true man: "Jesus Christ possesses two natures, one divine and the other human, not confused, but united in the one person of God's Son." Therefore, Saint Paul can write that in the fullness of time, "God sent forth his Son, born of woman" (Gal. 4:4).

And so at the appointed time, the eternal, divine Word of God (cf. Jn. 1:1), the Second Person of the Blessed Trinity, "became flesh and dwelt among us" (Jn. 1:14). Scripture teaches that Christ is Emmanuel—God is truly with us (cf. Mt. 1:23).

If we take these two biblical teachings, that (a) Mary is the mother of Jesus and (b) Jesus is truly God, then we must conclude that Mary is the mother of God. To conclude otherwise would be to deny either (a) or (b) or both, and thereby fall into one of the ancient heresies rejected by the apostolic Church.

What Is Motherhood?

To understand the Church's teaching on Mary's divine maternity, it is important to clarify what we mean by motherhood.

Motherhood is the relationship that is established when a woman communicates her own human nature to her children. This gift of nature occurs at conception, and is continually nurtured through gestation, childbirth, and the life of the child. At conception a human person, a real son or daughter—and not simply a physical body—comes into being. And this is true even though we know that the mother did not create the child's soul, which is created and infused directly by God.

Mary did not give Jesus His divine nature or His divine personhood, which was His from all eternity. Nor did she give Him His human soul, which was infused when He became man in her virginal womb (cf. Catechism, no. 471). As a true mother, Mary did give Jesus a human nature identical to her own, and she is the mother of a person, not merely a body or a nature.

Now here is the twist. In Jesus Christ, there are two natures—human and divine—and these natures are united without confusion in one divine Person, the Second Person of the Blessed Trinity, in what is called the *hypostatic union*. Since Mary is the mother of Jesus and Jesus is a divine Person—that is, God—then Mary is rightly called the "Mother of God."

There are two sonships, but only one Son. Christ is the true Son of God the Father from all eternity, but He is also the true Son of Mary, born in the fullness of time (cf. Gal. 4:4).

What About the Fathers?

Early Christian Tradition, particularly the liturgy, bears witness to the Christian belief that Mary is the Mother of God. In the oldest profession of the Christian faith, the Apostles' Creed (cf. Catechism, no. 194), the faithful for nearly two millennia have professed their faith in "Jesus Christ, His Only Son, Our Lord, who was conceived by the Holy Spirit, born of the Virgin Mary." The ancient Marian prayer *Sub tuum praesidium* ("We fly to thy protection . . ."), which dates back to the third century, explicitly addresses Mary as "Mother of God."

Mary's divine motherhood is richly attested to in the writings of the Church Fathers. For example, Saint Irenaeus (d. 202) wrote, "The Virgin Mary, . . . being obedient to His word, received from an angel the glad tidings that she would bear God."[1]

Saint Ephrem of Syria (d. 373), in his poetic *Hymns of the Nativity*, authored the following:

---

[1] Saint Irenaeus, *Against the Heresies*, 5, 19, 1, as quoted in William A. Jurgens, ed., *The Faith of the Early Fathers*, vol. 1 (Collegeville, MN: The Liturgical Press, 1970), 101.

In the womb of Mary, the Infant was formed,
who from eternity is equal to the Father. . . .
The Virgin became a Mother
while preserving her virginity;
And though still a virgin
she carried a Child in her womb;
And the handmaid and work of His Wisdom
became the Mother of God.[2]

Saint Athanasius (d. 373), in his treatise On the Incarnation of the Word of God and Against the Arians, wrote:

The Word begotten of the Father from on high, inexpressibly, inexplicably, incomprehensibly, and eternally, is He that is born in time here below, of the Virgin Mary, the Mother of God—so that those who are in the first place born here below might have a second birth from on high, that is, of God.[3]

These are just a handful of the many patristic references to this Marian teaching during the first four centuries of Christianity. Of course, after the dogmatic definition of the Council of Ephesus in 431 (see below), this teaching was firmly established as part of the deposit of faith entrusted to the Church (cf. 1 Tim. 6:20).

How Can We Go Wrong?
Historically, there have been three errors concerning Mary's divine maternity. First, some have held that Christ was true God, but not true man. Therefore, since Christ did not receive a human nature from Mary, she could not be called His mother.

The second error, much more prevalent today, is that Christ is truly a man, but not God. Therefore, Mary is truly the mother of Christ, but in no sense the mother of God.

The third error, called Nestorianism, is what occasioned the Church's definition at the Council of Ephesus. According to

---

[2] As quoted in ibid., vol. 1, 312.
[3] As quoted in ibid., vol. 1, 340.

this view, there were two persons in Christ, one divine and one human, and Mary gave birth only to the human person. She could rightly be called the Mother of Christ (*Christotokos*) or even the Receiver of God (*Theodokos*), but not the Mother of God (*Theotokos*).

Let's take a closer look at how this error was resolved by the Church.

Showdown at Ephesus

In his encyclical letter *On the 1500th Anniversary of the Council of Ephesus* (*Lux Veritatis*, 1931), Pope Pius XI traces the events leading up to the decisions of this ecumenical council.

Nestorius, a monk of Antioch who in 428 became the patriarch of Constantinople, publicly preached that Christ was not God, but that God only dwelt in Him as in a temple. In other words, he taught that there were two persons in Christ, and thus Mary was *Christotokos* (Mother of Christ), but not *Theotokos* (Mother of God). "*Christotokos*" became the watchword of the Nestorians.

The true Christian teaching was championed by Saint Cyril, who was the patriarch of Alexandria. Saint Cyril not only strenuously defended the Catholic faith among his own flock, but he also addressed letters to Nestorius in a charitable, brotherly attempt to lead him back to the Catholic faith.

When these attempts failed, Cyril appealed to Pope Celestine, writing that "[t]he ancient custom of the Churches admonishes us that matters of this kind should be communicated to Your Holiness."[4] Celestine condemned the teaching of Nestorius and appointed Cyril as his representative for settling the controversy.

Meanwhile, Emperor Theodosius convoked an ecumenical council at Ephesus to facilitate the resolution of the dispute. Under the presidency of Saint Cyril, and with full papal approval and authority, the Council condemned the false teaching of Nestorius and fully affirmed Christ's divinity:

---

[4] As quoted in *Lux Veritatis*, no. 12.

Scripture does not say that the Word associated the person of a man with Himself, but that He was made flesh. But when it is said that the Word was made flesh, that means nothing else but that He partook of flesh and blood, even as we do; wherefore, He made our body His own, and came forth man, born of a woman, at the same time without laying aside His Godhead, or His birth from the Father; for in assuming flesh He still remained what He was.[5]

The decision of the Council of Ephesus is a classic example of how authentic Marian doctrine flows from and will always protect and safeguard authentic teachings concerning the Person of Christ. By proclaiming that Mary is *Theotokos*, the Church is affirming that Mary is truly a mother, thus affirming Jesus' humanity. By affirming that she is the Mother of God, the Church is not only affirming Jesus' divinity, but also the union of Jesus' human and divine natures in His one divine Person.

Ecumenical Concerns
It is important to emphasize that the pronouncement of the Council of Ephesus, despite the necessary refutation of the Nestorian heresy, was a cause for rejoicing and celebration in the streets of Ephesus:

And the populace of Ephesus were drawn to the Virgin Mother of God with such great piety, and burning with such ardent love, that when they understood the judgment passed by the Fathers of the Council, they hailed them with overflowing gladness of heart, and gathering round them in a body, bearing lighted torches in their hands, accompanied them home.[6]

---

[5] As quoted in *ibid.*, no. 28; cf. Catechism, no. 466.
[6] *Ibid.*, no. 41.

To this day, devotion to the *Theotokos* is a point of unity among many Christians, particularly among the Eastern Orthodox Churches, as Vatican II teaches:

> It gives great joy and comfort to this sacred synod that among the separated brethren too there are those who give due honor to the Mother of Our Lord and Savior, especially among the Easterns, who with devout mind and fervent impulse give honor to the Mother of God, ever virgin (LG 69).

Among Protestant Christians in the West, there are diverse views concerning Mary's role in the work of salvation (UR 20). Interestingly, the three fathers of the Protestant Reformation—Luther, Calvin, and Zwingli—all affirmed Mary's divine maternity.

"All generations will call me blessed" (Lk. 1:48)

The Church has, from the earliest times, honored Mary with the title "Mother of God" (Catechism, no. 971). Because of her intimate, mother-Son relationship with the Redeemer of the world, the Church recognizes her "high office" and "dignity," as well as the fact that she is also "the beloved daughter of the Father and the temple of the Holy Spirit" (LG 53).

In a singular but subordinate way, she freely cooperated in her Son's saving work by her obedience, faith, hope, and burning charity (LG 61). She is our mother in the order of grace, the new mother of all those who are alive in Christ (cf. Gen. 3:20), the mother of all of Christ's beloved disciples (cf. Jn. 19:27), who keep the commandments and bear witness to Him (cf. Rev. 12:17).

For that reason, the Church honors Mary "with filial affection and devotion as a most beloved mother" (LG 53). This devotion is not the adoration that is proper to God alone, but rather the love for a mother who always reminds us to follow her Son (cf. Jn. 2:5), so that He may be known, loved, and glorified, and that all people may be gathered into one family in Christ, to the glory of the Most Holy Trinity.

_____*SideBar*____

The Protestant Reformers on Mary

Martin Luther: "In this work whereby she was made the Mother of God, so many and such good things were given her that no one can grasp them. . . . Not only was Mary the mother of Him who is born [in Bethlehem], but of Him who, before the world, was eternally born of the Father, from a Mother in time and at the same time man and God."

John Calvin: "It cannot be denied that God in choosing and destining Mary to be the Mother of His Son, granted her the highest honor. . . . Elizabeth calls Mary Mother of the Lord, because the unity of the person in the two natures of Christ was such that she could have said that the mortal man engendered in the womb of Mary was at the same time the eternal God."

Ulrich Zwingli: "It was given to her what belongs to no creature, that in the flesh she should bring forth the Son of God."

—As quoted in *Beginning Apologetics:*
How to Explain and Defend the Catholic Faith
(Farmington, NM: San Juan Catholic Seminars, 1993-96)

Questions for Reflection
or Group Discussion

1. What was decided at the Council of Ephesus? How does the title "Mother of God" preserve an orthodox understanding of who Jesus Christ is?

2. Since Mary is never called the "Mother of God" in the Bible, how can I explain this title to a Christian who rejects the authority of the Church?

3. Jesus is the "first-born among many brethren" (Rom. 8:29). If I am Jesus' brother or sister, what should my attitude be toward Jesus' mother? Toward other Christians?

Chapter 22

MARY, CONCEIVED WITHOUT SIN
The Dogma of the Immaculate Conception

What is the Immaculate Conception? Is the Church's teaching on the Immaculate Conception biblical?

The dogma of the Immaculate Conception, as solemnly defined by Pope Pius IX in 1854, teaches that

> the most Blessed Virgin Mary, in the first instant of her conception, by a singular grace and privilege granted by Almighty God, in view of the merits of Jesus Christ, the Savior of the human race, was preserved free from all stain of original sin.[1]

This means that Mary, through the merits of her Son and Savior, Jesus Christ, received a special grace so that she might become the spiritual mother of all who come to believe in her divine Son (cf. Gen. 3:20; Jn. 19:26-27; Rev. 12:17).

Mary's Immaculate Conception should be seen as the way God wanted all of us to come into the world: in the state of sanctifying grace and free from original sin, just like Adam and Eve.

> God's original plan was for all humans to begin their existence in the family of God in the state of sanctifying grace. It was only as a result of Original Sin that we are now conceived in a state deprived of sanctifying grace. Mary, rather than being the exception, fulfills in a real sense the original intention of what God wanted for all His human children: to be members of His family from the first moment of their existence.[2]

---

[1] Apostolic Constitution *Ineffabilis Deus* (1854) (Boston, MA: St. Paul Books & Media), 21.
[2] Mark Miravalle, *Introduction to Mary* (Santa Barbara, CA: Queenship Publishing Co., 1993), 42.

Scriptural Evidence

Scripture, not coincidentally, first teaches the doctrine of Mary's Immaculate Conception in the Book of Genesis. Just after the sin of our first parents, God promised to send a Savior. Speaking to the serpent, God said, "I will put enmity between you and the woman, and between your seed and her seed; he shall bruise your head, and you shall bruise his heel" (Gen. 3:15).

The serpent is Satan (cf. Jn. 8:44; Rev. 12:9), and the "seed of the woman" who would be sent to crush the devil is Jesus Christ. Therefore, the "woman" is Mary, His mother. It is significant that Jesus addresses His mother in the Gospels as "woman" (e.g., Jn. 2:4; 19:26-27). Mary shares in the victory of her Son over Satan, which includes His victory over sin and death. Because she is sinless and pure, there is indeed "enmity" (Gen. 3:15) or "complete opposition" between Mary and Satan.

At the Annunciation, Saint Gabriel the Archangel greets Mary with the words, "Hail, full of grace, the Lord is with you" (Lk. 1:28). The phrase "full of grace" is a translation of the Greek word *kecharitōménē*. This word conveys a sense of completion and perfection that was already present at the time of the Annunciation. Mary's holiness was not only as complete as possible, but it extended over the whole of her life, from conception onward.

From this it follows that

> the Immaculate Conception means that Mary, whose conception was brought about the normal way, was conceived in the womb of her mother without the stain of original sin. The essence of original sin consists in the lack of sanctifying grace. Mary was preserved from this defect; from the first instant of her existence she was in the state of sanctifying grace.[3]

---

[3] Karl Keating, *Catholicism and Fundamentalism* (San Francisco: Ignatius Press, 1988), 270.

Mother of the Redeemer

In his 1986 encyclical on Mary as Mother of the Redeemer, Pope John Paul II teaches that "the messenger greets Mary as 'full of grace'; he calls her thus as if it were her real name. He does not call her by her proper earthly name: Miryam (= Mary), but by *this new name: 'full of grace'*" (RMT 8). "According to the belief formulated in solemn documents of the Church," the Pope adds,

> this "glory of grace" is manifested in the Mother of God through the fact that she has been "redeemed in a more sub-lime manner." By virtue of the richness of the grace of the beloved Son, by reason of the redemptive merits of him who willed to become her Son, Mary was *preserved from the inheritance of original sin.* In this way, from the first moment of her conception—which is to say of her existence—she belonged to Christ, sharing in the salvific and sanctifying grace and in that love which has its beginning in the "Beloved, " the Son of the Eternal Father, who through the Incarnation became her own Son (RMT 10, footnotes omitted).

Church Fathers

In the fourth century, Saint Ephrem the Syrian (d. 373), a doctor of the Church, composed this beautiful hymn:

> You alone and your Mother
>   are more beautiful than any others;
> For there is no blemish in you,
>   nor any stains upon your Mother.
> Who of my children
>   can compare in beauty to these?[4]

---

[4] Saint Ephrem the Syrian, *The Nisibine Hymns*, 27, 8, as quoted in William A. Jurgens, ed., *The Faith of the Early Fathers*, vol. 2 (Collegeville, MN: The Liturgical Press, 1979), 721.

On the issue of Mary's sinlessness and fullness of grace, Saint Augustine (d. 430) wrote:

> With the exception of the holy Virgin Mary, in whose case, out of respect for the Lord, I do not wish there to be any further question as far as sin is concerned, since how can we know what great abundance of grace was conferred on her to conquer sin in every way, seeing that she merited to conceive and bear him who certainly had no sin at all?[5]

Many other early Christians bore witness to Mary's freedom from sin, a freedom that allowed her to embrace wholeheartedly the Father's unique mission for her with complete openness. For example, Saint Gregory of Nazianzen (d. 390), Saint Gregory of Nyssa (d. 395), Saint Sophronius (d. 638), and Saint John Damascene (d. c. 749) among others taught that Mary was preserved from all stain of sin.

Saint Severus (d. 538), Bishop of Antioch in the sixth century, reflected on Mary in light of Sacred Tradition and Sacred Scripture: "She [Mary] . . . formed part of the human race, and was of the same essence as we, although she was pure from all taint and immaculate."[6] Saint Ambrose (d. 379), another early Church Father, referred to Mary as "free of every stain of sin."[7] Saint Andrew of Crete (d. 740) explained that the Redeemer chose "in all nature this pure and entirely Immaculate Virgin."[8] Thus, from the early centuries of the Church, Mary was seen as unique in her sinlessness.

---

[5] Saint Augustine, De Natura et Gratia, 36, 42; PL 44, 267, as quoted in Luigi Gambero, S.M., Mary and the Fathers of the Church (San Francisco: Ignatius Press, 1999), 226.
[6] Saint Severus, Hom. cathedralis, 67, Patrologia Orientalis (PO) 8, 350, as quoted in Miravalle, 40.
[7] Saint Ambrose of Milan, Commentary on Psalm 118, 22, 30, as quoted in Jurgens, vol. 2, 166.
[8] Saint Andrew of Crete, Hom. 1 in Nativ. Deiparae, PG 97, 913-14, as quoted in Miravalle, 40.

The New Eve

Because of the disobedience of Adam and Eve, all of their descendants fell from grace and are held in the bondage of sin. One of the effects of this original sin is our weakened freedom (cf. Rom. 7:14). Because of the special grace bestowed on her by God "in the fullness of time" (Gal. 4:4), Mary was preserved from enslavement to sin. Therefore, she was able to exercise her freedom completely in choosing to say "yes" to God. Her *fiat*— "Let it be to me according to your word" (Lk. 1:38)—is complete and wholehearted. Her "yes," given with full integrity, completely reverses Eve's "no."

Saint Irenaeus (d. 202) summed this up, writing that "the knot of Eve's disobedience was untied by Mary's obedience; what the virgin Eve bound through her disbelief, Mary loosened by her faith" (as quoted in LG 56).

Given to all of Jesus' disciples on the Cross (cf. Jn. 19:26; Rev. 12:17), Mary from the earliest times has been called the New Eve, the new "mother of all the living" (Gen. 3:20), who cooperated with Jesus, the New Adam (cf. Rom. 5:12-21), in saving the human family. As Saint Jerome wrote in the fifth century, "[D]eath through Eve, life through Mary" (as quoted in LG 56).

To prepare her for her role as the mother of the Savior, Mary "was enriched by God with gifts appropriate to such a role" (LG 56). More than anyone else, Mary was blessed "in Christ with every spiritual blessing in the heavenly places" (Eph. 1:3). The Father chose her in Christ before the foundation of the world to be holy and blameless before Him in love (cf. Eph. 1:4; Catechism, no. 492).

Mary's Immaculate Conception helped fulfill God's plan that He had from the beginning for all human beings. He was preparing her to be the most worthy cooperator with her divine Son in His mission to the world, as the New Eve with the New Adam, Jesus Christ.

Saved by Christ

Some might object that the Bible says that "all have sinned" (Rom. 3:23), and thus are in need of redemption by Christ. But "all" can mean "the great many" as opposed to each

and every person. Indeed, babies who die before the age of reason necessarily could not have committed personal sins; they
only could have suffered from the stain of original sin.
Meanwhile, Mary, the New Eve, was saved by Christ from the
instant of her conception and thus was preserved from the
effects of original sin:

> It took a positive act of God to keep her from coming under
> [original sin's] effects the way we have. We had the stain of
> original sin removed through baptism, which brings sanctify-
> ing grace to the soul, thus making the soul spiritually alive and
> capable of enjoying heaven, and makes the recipient a mem-
> ber of the Church. We might say that Mary received a very
> special kind of "baptism" at her conception, but, because since
> she never contracted original sin, she enjoyed certain privi-
> leges we never can, such as entire avoidance of sin.[9]

My Son, the Doctor

As Blessed Duns Scotus (d. 1308), known as the "Marian
Doctor," explained, "Mary would greatly have needed Christ as
a Redeemer, for she would have contracted original sin by reason of human propagation unless she had been preserved
through the grace of the Mediator."[10] In other words, what we
receive as a "remedy" through the Sacrament of Baptism, Mary
by a special grace received by way of "inoculation" through the
merits of the Divine Physician.

Mary's Immaculate Conception, then, is a biblical teaching
that shows forth the wonders of the salvation offered to us in
Christ. This most beautiful handiwork of God—Mary—at the
very moment of her conception, was preserved from sin by the
Cross of her beloved Son. If the saving events of Calvary can
be applied to someone 2,000 years after the event, then the
eternal God can apply those same merits to Mary to preserve
her from the ravages of original sin, and thus prepare her as a
more fitting tabernacle for the Son of God.

---

[9] Keating, 271.
[10] Blessed Duns Scotus, *In 3 sent.*, 18.13, as quoted in *New Catholic Encyclopedia*, vol. 4
(Washington: The Catholic University of America, 1967), 1105.

Questions for Reflection
or Group Discussion

1. Have I ever confused the Immaculate Conception with Jesus' conception? What is the Church's teaching on the Immaculate Conception? (See Catechism, nos. 490-93.) The Church's calendar helps in this regard:

December 8 Immaculate Conception (Mary conceived)	March 25 Annunciation (Jesus conceived)
9 months later . . . September 8 Birth of Mary	9 months later . . . December 25 Birth of Jesus

2. Explain how Mary was "saved" by Jesus. How would I respond to the charge that the Immaculate Conception detracts from the glory of God?

3. Mary used her freedom to say "yes" wholeheartedly to God's plan for her life. What can I do to submit more completely to God's will for me?

Chapter 23

WHAT'S A MOTHER TO DO?
Mary's Role in Our Salvation

What is Mary's role in our salvation? Isn't Jesus Christ the one Mediator between God and man?

Mary's role can be summarized by the terms Coredemptrix, Mediatrix, and Advocate (cf. Catechism, no. 969). Mary's maternal role in our salvation, as summarized by these titles, is part of the constant teaching of the Church.

Saint Paul teaches us that "there is one mediator between God and men, the man Christ Jesus, who gave himself as a ransom for all" (1 Tim. 2:5). Mary's participation in salvation history as Mother of Christ and Mother of Christians does not diminish the unique mediation of Christ; rather, it points to Christ's unique mediation and reveals its power (LG 60).

In recent years there has been increased speculation as to whether the Church will dogmatically define Mary's role as Coredemptrix, Mediatrix, and Advocate. Whether the Church ultimately does so or not, we are called to "think with the Church" and understand the rock-solid doctrine behind the titles. Some people object to these titles, particularly to Mary's being considered "Coredemptrix" and "Mediatrix," because they think the titles somehow detract from Christ. Yet, just as human fathers participate in the one Fatherhood of God, and priests participate in the one priesthood of Christ, so also God has chosen to associate Mary in a unique way with Christ's one mediation.

Mary's pivotal role in salvation history did not end with her giving birth to the Son of God, but rather continues to the present time. If we were to take 1 Timothy 2:5 (above) in a sense that bars the participation of others in Christ's mediation, then we would have to admit that we should not ask anybody to pray for us, nor should we pray for others. But that is an unbiblical position! If we acknowledge that we can pray for each other as members of the Body of Christ (e.g., 1 Thess. 5:25; 2 Thess. 1:11), then surely we would want the prayers of the woman whom all generations call blessed (Lk. 1:48). After all, not even death can separate the members of God's family (cf. Rom. 8:38-39).

Coredemptrix

The title "Coredemptrix" is a term that refers to Mary's unique and intimate cooperation with her divine Son in redeeming the human family. The title is rooted in Genesis 3:15, where Mary is "prophetically foreshadowed in the promise of victory over the serpent" (LG 55). This passage foreshadows the divine work of redemption brought about by Jesus as the Savior of the world, with the *Mother of the Redeemer's intimate cooperation.*

The prefix "co" in the title "Coredemptrix" does not imply an equality with the one Redeemer, Jesus Christ, who alone could reconcile humanity with the Father in His divinity and humanity. The prefix "co" is derived from the Latin word *cum*, which means "with," and not "equal to." Jesus as true God and true man redeems the human family, and Mary as "Coredemptrix" participates with the divine Redeemer in a completely subordinate and dependent way. Nonetheless, though subordinate and dependent, Mary's human participation remains a uniquely privileged and exalted one, one that was entirely contingent upon her free and meritorious "yes" in her words, "[L]et it be to me according to your word" (Lk. 1:38).

As explained by Pope John Paul II:

> Crucified spiritually with her crucified Son (cf. Gal. 2:20), she contemplated with heroic love the death of her God, she "lovingly consented to the immolation of this Victim which she herself had brought forth" (LG 58) . . . as she was in a special way close to the Cross of her Son, she also had to have a privileged experience of his Resurrection. In fact, Mary's role as co-redemptrix did not cease with the glorification of her Son.[1]

---

[1] Pope John Paul II, "Allocution at the Sanctuary of Our Lady of Alborada in Quayaquil" (January 31, 1985), as reported in *L'Osservatore Romano* (English ed., March 11, 1985), 7.

Through faith and Baptism, we become God's children by adoption and participate in the divine life. As new creations in Christ, we cooperate in His redemptive work. While this is true of all Christians, it is most perfectly true of Mary, who was never wounded or enslaved by sin and therefore was perfectly free to give herself completely to Christ.

Mediatrix of All Graces

Mary is called "Mediatrix" (Catechism, no. 969) because all grace comes from Christ, and Christ comes only through Mary by the power of the Holy Spirit.

Mary is also known as the "Mother of all Christians." This title refers to Our Lord's words from the Cross to Mary and John (Jn. 19:26-27). At the time of His death, Jesus gave Mary to John and John to Mary. "From that hour [John] took her to his own home" (Jn. 19:27). John represented the Church at the foot of the Cross. Therefore, all of us are invited to welcome Mary into our homes as our mother.

The Holy Spirit makes this point again through Saint John in Revelation 12:17, when "the woman," the mother of the Redeemer, is also described as the mother of all who keep the commandments of God and hold to the testimony of Jesus. God chose to save us by becoming man and allowing the Blessed Virgin to be His mother. Our salvation comes by being grafted into the Family of God by faith and Baptism. In a family, the mother is necessary, and so Mary in this sense is necessary for salvation.

In Jesus' one and perfect mediation (cf. 1 Tim. 2:5), subordinate and secondary mediators are able to participate. In the Old Testament, God used the patriarchs and prophets to mediate His reconciliation with the people of Israel. In the Old and New Testaments, God used angels to mediate His messages and His grace. Vatican II teaches that after Mary was taken up into heaven, "she did not lay aside this saving office but by her manifold intercession continues to bring us the gifts of eternal salvation" (LG 62).

Saint Paul says that all Christians are mediators or "ambassadors for Christ" (2 Cor. 5:18-20), sent and entrusted by Christ's authority to mediate God's message of reconciliation.

Those who receive these ambassadors receive Christ Himself: "[H]e who receives any one whom I send receives me; and he who receives me receives him who sent me" (Jn. 13:20; cf. Lk. 10:16; Mt. 10:40).

Mary participates in the mediation of Christ in a way unlike any other creature. In John 2, her mediation at the wedding of Cana led to the first public miracle and the beginning of Jesus' public ministry. In Luke 1:41, her physical mediation brings the unborn Jesus to His unborn cousin, John the Baptist, who is sanctified in Elizabeth's womb. So through Mary's mediation, and her active participation with God's grace, Christ is brought to others. The Fathers of the Church recognized her role as Mediatrix. For example, Saint Ephrem in the fourth century referred to her as "the Mediatrix of the whole world."[2]

Although the teaching on Mary's role as Mediatrix is not dogmatically defined, it is nevertheless part of the Church's constant teaching. The following popes speak of Mary as Mediatrix of all graces: Pope Pius VII, Pope Pius IX, Pope Leo XIII, Pope St. Pius X, Pope Benedict XV, Pope Pius XI, Pope Pius XII, Pope John XXIII, Pope Paul VI, and Pope John Paul II.[3]

The very first verse of the New Testament introduces Jesus to the world as "Son of Abraham, Son of David" (Mt. 1:1). As Son of David, Jesus is the King of Israel. All the kings in Jerusalem had a queen, but she was not their wife. Rather, the queen was their mother. Scripture tells us that King Solomon, for example, had 700 wives and 300 concubines. The queen was shown devotion by all—even the king (1 Kings 2:19)—and sat in the king's presence to make intercession for the people. Since Mary is alive in Christ, she lives to intercede for her children.[4]

---

[2] Saint Ephrem, *Ad Deiparam*, Oratio IV, as quoted in Mark Miravalle, *Introduction to Mary* (Santa Barbara, CA: Queenship Publishing Co., 1993), 67.

[3] See Miravalle, 74-80.

[4] For further discussion of Mary's role as Queen Mother, see Timothy Gray, "Scripture's Revelation of Mary," published in Hahn and Suprenant, eds., *Catholic for a Reason: Scripture and the Mystery of the Family of God* (Steubenville, OH: Emmaus Road Publishing, 1998), 193-99.

Mary, Our Advocate

This leads to the third title of Mary, that of "Advocate for the People of God." The early Church manifested her heartfelt belief in the intercessory power of Mary, to whom she called for help and protection in the midst of dangers and trials. The *Salve Regina* (Hail Holy Queen), composed in the eleventh century, includes this venerable title. Vatican II continues this ancient practice of invoking Mary under the title that conveys her role as intercessory helper for the People of God in times of peril: "Therefore the Blessed Virgin is invoked in the Church under the [title] of Advocate[.] . . ." (LG 62).

We can therefore say that the Coredemptrix, who uniquely participated with the one Redeemer in obtaining the graces of redemption, continues her participation by distributing the graces of redemption with the one Mediator, Jesus Christ, and the Sanctifier, the Holy Spirit. Part of this mediating role of Mary in God's plan of salvation includes the providential task of being the Advocate for the People of God, that is, a mother pleading on behalf of her children. Thus Mary not only mediates the graces of God to humanity as Mediatrix, but she also mediates the petitions of the human family back to God as our Advocate.

Church Teaching

In his apostolic letter *Tertio Millennio Adveniente* (The Coming Third Millennium), Pope John Paul II tells us that "Mary in fact constantly points to her Divine Son and she is proposed to all believers as the *model of faith* which is put into practice" (no. 43, original emphasis). The role of Mary as Coredemptrix offers us the rich ecclesial model of our becoming coworkers (cf. 1 Cor. 3:9) or *coredeemers in Christ.* Since she is the preeminent model of the Church, every revealed truth about Mary provides the Church inspiration and wisdom in her quest to "conquer sin and increase in holiness" (LG 65).

The Marian model of Coredemptrix offers a particular richness to the Church regarding the Christian call to be coredeemers in Christ, based on Saint Paul's exhortation to every Christian to "make up what is lacking in the sufferings of Christ, for the sake of the body, which is the Church" (Col. 1:24). The preeminent example of this scriptural call of cooperation in the work of redemption is most certainly Mary Coredemptrix. "Coredeemers in Christ" as a description of the Family of God echoes the compelling Vatican II theme that calls every Christian to bring Christ to the world and to collaborate with the Redeemer in bringing the graces of salvation to all peoples today.

Mary's coredemptive example is a constant reminder to the faithful that we must all work alongside the Redeemer in bringing the saving Gospel of Christ into the world; to offer our meritorious sufferings for the glory of God and the salvation of souls in the order of the priesthood of the laity, as well as in the ministerial priesthood; to participate through acts of charity and Christian works of mercy in the application of the graces of Calvary to the world today, a world that remains in such grave need of the Redeemer's spiritual and social liberation; to realize the sublime ecclesial dignity of freely and personally cooperating with grace for our own salvation and the salvation of all humanity; and to be incarnate witnesses after the model of Mary Coredemptrix to the fundamental truth that human suffering can be redemptive.

Our role as "coredeemers in Christ" provides a concrete reminder to today's faithful that the Cross of the Redeemer must again be implanted in the midst of the world and carried by *every beloved disciple* for the salvation and sanctification of contemporary society.

Mary is the "dawn" before Christ the "Day," for the Father willed that the mother precede the incarnate Son in the history of salvation. And, as the announcement of the motherhood of Mary by the angel Gabriel preceded and prepared for the Incarnation, so one can see the profound significance of deepening our understanding of Mary's maternal mediation as we celebrate the third millennium of Christ's Incarnation.

May the Holy Spirit guide the Church in her reflection on Mary's role in our salvation, and enable the People of God to listen attentively to what the Spirit is "saying to the Churches" (cf. Rev. 2:7) today about our common mother (RMT 30). May we do our part in fulfilling the great Marian prophecy inspired by the same Spirit that "all generations will call [Mary] blessed" (Lk. 1:48).

Questions for Reflection
or Group Discussion

1. How would I explain Mary's role as "Coredemptrix" to a Christian who doesn't accept the teaching authority of the Church? What pitfalls must be avoided?

2. Read Catechism, no. 970. How does the concept of "participation" help me to understand Mary's mediation?

3. Do I understand Mary to be my Advocate? Do I entrust my cares and petitions to her? How can I deepen my relationship with the Blessed Mother?

RECOMMENDED REFERENCES

General
Ignatius Bible (Ignatius Press, Revised Standard Version,
    Catholic Edition)
Catechism of the Catholic Church
Austin Flannery, O.P., ed., *Vatican II: The Conciliar and Post
    Conciliar Documents*, vols. 1 and 2 (Costello Publishing Co.)
Précis of Official Catholic Teaching (Catholics Committed to
    Support the Pope, eleven-volume set)
Code of Canon, Law Latin-English Edition
    (Canon Law Society of America)
William A. Jurgens, ed., *The Faith of the Early Fathers*
    (The Liturgical Press, three-volume set)
Scott Hahn and Leon Suprenant, eds., *Catholic for a Reason:
    Scripture and the Mystery of the Family of God*
    (Emmaus Road Publishing)
Peter M.J. Stravinskas, *A Tour of the Catechism*
    (Marytown Press)
Henry Denzinger, ed., *The Sources of Catholic Dogma*
    (Marian House, trans. by Roy Deferrari)
Eusebius, *The History of the Church* (Viking Penguin)
Mike Aquilina, *The Fathers of the Church: An Introduction
    to the First Christian Teachers* (Our Sunday Visitor)

Doctrine and Liturgy
Pope Paul VI, *Mysterium Fidei* (On the Holy Eucharist)
Pope John Paul II, *Ordinatio Sacerdotalis*
    (On Reserving Priestly Ordination to Men Alone)
Pope John Paul II, *Tertio Millennio Adveniente*
    (On Preparation for the Jubilee of the Year 2000)
Pope John Paul II, *Dominicae Cenae*
    (The Mystery and Worship of the Eucharist)

Pope John Paul II, *Vicesimus Quintus Annus* (On the 25th
   Anniversary of the Constitution *Sacrosanctum Concilium*)
Sacred Congregation of Rites, *Eucharisticum Mysterium*
   (Instruction on the Worship of the Eucharistic Mystery)
Sacred Congregation for the Sacraments and Divine Worship,
   Inaestimabile Donum (Instruction Concerning Worship of
   the Eucharistic Mystery)
Instruction from various dicasteries of the Apostolic See,
   *Instruction on Certain Questions Concerning the Collaboration
   of the Lay Faithful in the Ministry of Priests*
Congregation of Rites, *Tres Abhinc Annos* (Second Instruction
   on the Proper Implementation of the Constitution of the
   Sacred Liturgy)
Sacred Congregation for Divine Worship, *Liturgiae Instaurationes*
   (Third Instruction on the Correct Implementation of the
   Constitution on the Sacred Liturgy)
Sacred Congregation for Divine Worship, *General Instruction
   on the Roman Missal* (GIRM) fourth edition, 1975
Frank Sheed, *Theology for Beginners* (Servant Books)
James T. O'Connor, *The Hidden Manna* (Ignatius Press)
Mark P. Shea, *This Is My Body* (Christendom Press)
Karl Keating, *What Catholics Really Believe* (Ignatius Press)
Russell Shaw, ed., *Encyclopedia of Catholic Doctrine*
   (Our Sunday Visitor)
Michael L. Gaudoin-Parker, *The Real Presence Through the Ages*
   (Alba House)
Alfred McBride, O.Praem., *Essentials of the Faith*
   (Our Sunday Visitor)
St. Athanasius, *On the Incarnation* (St. Vladimir Seminary
   Press edition)
Scott Hahn, *Growth By Oath: The Seven Sacraments*
   (audiotape set) (St. Joseph Communications, Inc.)
Scott Hahn, *Eucharistic Day at Marytown* (audiotape set)
   (St. Joseph Communications, Inc.)
Scott Hahn, *Corpus Christi: A Father's Day Celebration*
   (audiotape set) (St. Joseph Communications, Inc.)
Benedict Groeschel, C.F.R., and James Monti,
   In the Presence of Our Lord (Our Sunday Visitor)

Peter J. Elliott, *Ceremonies of the Modern Roman Rite*
(Ignatius Press)
Joan Carroll Cruz, *Eucharistic Miracles* (Tan Publisher)
Mary Ann Budnik, *Looking for Peace? Try Confession* (RB Media)

Morality and Marriage & Family
Pope Paul VI, *Humanae Vitae* (On the Regulation of Birth)
Pope Pius XI, *Casti Connubii* (On Christian Marriage)
Pope Leo XIII, *Arcanum* (On Christian Marriage)
Pope John Paul II, *Evangelium Vitae* (On the Value and
    Inviolability of Human Life)
Pope John Paul II, *Veritatis Splendor* (Regarding Certain
    Fundamental Questions of the Church's Moral Teaching)
Pope John Paul II, *Familiaris Consortio* (On the Role of the
    Christian Family in the Modern World)
Pope John Paul II, *Gratissimum Sane* (Letter to Families)
Pope John Paul II, *The Theology of the Body: Human Love in the
    Divine Plan* (Pauline Books & Media)
Pontifical Council for the Family, *Vademecum for Confessors
    Concerning Some Aspects of the Morality of Conjugal Life*
Congregation for the Doctrine of the Faith, *Declaration on
    Certain Questions Concerning Sexual Ethics*
Germain Grisez, *The Way of the Lord Jesus* (Franciscan Press,
    three-volume set)
Romanus Cessario, O.P., *The Moral Virtues and Theological Ethics*
    (University of Notre Dame Press)
Karol Wojtyla, *Love and Responsibility* (Ignatius Press)
Thomas Williams, L.C., *Building on Solid Ground* (Alba House)
Archbishop Fulton Sheen, *Three to Get Married* (Scepter Press)
Frederick Marks, *The Catholic Handbook for Engaged and Newly
    Married Couples* (Faith Publishing)
Dietrich von Hildebrand, *Marriage, the Mystery of Faithful Love*
    (Sophia Institute Press)
Curtis Martin, *Restoring the Hearts of Fathers* (audiotape set)
    (Emmaus Road Publishing)
Curtis Martin, Philip Gray, and Marcus Grodi, *Safeguarding the
    Family* (audiotape set) (Emmaus Road Publishing)
Dom Hubert Van Zeller, *Holiness for Housewives* (and other
    working women) (Sophia Institute Press)

Mercedes Wilson, *Love and Family: Raising a Traditional Family in a Secular World* (Ignatius Press)

Janet E. Smith, ed., *Why Humanae Vitae Was Right: A Reader* (Ignatius Press)

Janet E. Smith, *Humanae Vitae: A Challenge to Love by Pope Paul VI* (New Hope Publications)

Janet E. Smith, *Humanae Vitae, A Generation Later* (Catholic University of America Press)

John F. Kippley, *Marriage Is for Keeps* (Couple to Couple League)

John F. Kippley, *Sex and the Marriage Covenant* (Couple to Couple League)

John F. Kippley, *Birth Control and Christian Discipleship* (Couple to Couple League)

John and Sheila Kippley, *Art of Natural Family Planning* (Couple to Couple League; fourth edition)

Sheila Kippley, *Breastfeeding and Natural Child Spacing* (Couple to Couple League)

William D. Virtue, *Mother and Infant* (Pontifical University of St. Thomas Aquinas, Rome)

G.K. Chesterton, *Brave New Family* (Ignatius Press)

Donald DeMarco, *Biotechnology and the Assault on Parenthood* (Ignatius Press)

William E. May, *Marriage: The Rock on Which the Family Is Built* (Ignatius Press)

Scott and Kimberly Hahn, *Becoming a Catholic Family* (audiotape set) (St. Joseph Communications, Inc.)

Rick and Jan Hess, *A Full Quiver* (Wolgemuth and Hyatt Publishers, Inc.)

Stephen Wood with James Burnham, *Christian Fatherhood* (Family Life Center Publications)

Peter J. Elliott, *What God Has Joined . . . The Sacramentality of Marriage* (Alba House)

Catholic Education

Pope John Paul II, *Catechesi Tradendae* (On Catechesis in Our Time)

Pope Paul VI, *Credo of the People of God*

Pope St. Pius X, *Catechism of Catholic Doctrine*

Pontifical Council for the Family, *The Truth and Meaning of Human Sexuality*
Congregation for Catholic Education, *Educational Guidance in Human Love*
Faith and Life elementary catechism series (Ignatius Press, for more information call Benedictus Books toll-free at 1-888-316-2640)
Congregation for the Clergy, *General Directory for Catechesis*
Catholicism high school catechism series (C.R. Publications, 4-volume set)
Kimberly Hahn and Mary Hasson, *Catholic Education: Homeward Bound* (Ignatius Press)
Michael J. Wrenn and Kenneth D. Whitehead, *Flawed Expectations* (Ignatius Press)

Apologetics and Mary
Pope Leo XIII, *Providentissimus Deus* (On the Study of Holy Scripture)
Pope Benedict XV, *Spiritus Paraclitus* (On the Fifteenth Centenary of the Death of St. Jerome)
Pope Pius XII, *Divino Afflante Spiritu* (On Promoting Biblical Studies)
Pope John Paul II, *Redemptoris Mater* (Mother of the Redeemer)
Curtis Martin and Patrick Madrid, *Winning Souls, Not Just Arguments* (audiotape set) (Emmaus Road Publishing)
Patrick Madrid, *Any Friend of God's Is a Friend of Mine* (Basilica Press)
Patrick Madrid, ed., *Surprised by Truth* (Basilica Press)
Tim Gray, *Mission of the Messiah* (Emmaus Road Publishing)
Scott Hahn, *Answering Common Objections* (audiotape set) (St. Joseph Communications, Inc.)
Scott Hahn, *Can You Trust the Bible?* (audiotape set) (St. Joseph Communications, Inc.)
Scott Hahn, *A New Look at Our Lady* (audiotape set) (St. Joseph Communications, Inc.)
Karl Keating, *Catholicism and Fundamentalism* (Ignatius Press)
David Currie, *Born Fundamentalist, Born Again Catholic* (Ignatius Press)

Mark P. Shea, *By What Authority?* (Our Sunday Visitor)
Leslie Rumble and Charles Carty, *Radio Replies*, vols. 1-3
    (Tan Books and Publishers)
Mark Miravalle, *Introduction to Mary: The Heart of Marian
    Doctrine and Devotion* (Queenship Press)
Scott Hahn, *A Father Who Keeps His Promises* (Servant Books)
Luigi Gambero, S.M., *Mary and the Fathers of the Church*
    (Ignatius Press)

**To obtain any of these resources, call Benedictus Books
toll-free at 1-888-316-2640 (CUF members receive a 10%
discount), or visit the Catholic bookstore in your area.**

Other Available FAITH FACTS

CREED
St. Augustine's Real Faith in the Real Presence
The Human Knowledge of Christ
It "Works" for Me: The Church's Teaching on Justification
Purgatory
Indulgences
Limbo?

LITURGY
Signs of the Christ: Sacraments of the Catholic Church
Eucharistic Consecration: Kneeling or Standing?
Reception of Holy Communion
Ordinary and Extraordinary Eucharistic Ministers
First Confession/First Communion
I Confess: The Biblical Basis of the Sacrament of Reconciliation

MORALITY
The Necessity of Law and Right Order
Following Our Bishops
Canonical Misconception: Pope Pius IX and the Church's
    Teaching on Abortion
Withholding Nutrition and Hydration:
    Influences of the Culture of Death

CATHOLIC EDUCATION AND FAMILY
Parental Rights and Chastity Education:
    Working Within the Church to Resolve Concerns
The Annulment Process
Home Schooling Resources
What Makes a Marriage?: Consent, Consummation,
    and the Special Case of the Holy Family

BIBLICAL APOLOGETICS
What's in a Name?: Protocanon, Deuterocanon, Apocrypha
The Complete Bible: Why Catholics Have Seven More Books
"Call No Man Father"?: Understanding Matthew 23:9

MARY
Mary's Perpetual Virginity
The Assumption of the Blessed Virgin Mary
Honor Thy Mother: Praising Mary and the Saints
    Is Biblically Correct
Rock Solid: Salvation History of the Catholic Church

FAITH FACTS are a free membership service of Catholics
United for the Faith. For more information, write Catholics
United for the Faith, 827 North Fourth St., Steubenville, OH
43952; call 1-800-MY-FAITH (693-2484); or visit CUF's
website at www.cuf.org.

EFFECTIVE LAY WITNESS PROTOCOL

By reason of the knowledge, competence or pre-eminence which they have the laity are empowered—indeed sometimes obliged—to manifest their opinion on those things which pertain to the good of the Church. If the occasion should arise this should be done through the institutions established by the Church for that purpose and always with truth, courage and prudence and with reverence and charity toward those who, by reason of their office, represent the person of Christ (LG 37).

To assist the faithful when controversies arise, the Church has provided certain procedures. These procedures respect the "institutions established by the Church" and are set forth in the Code of Canon Law. There are three types of procedures that can be used: judicial, administrative, and pastoral. In all circumstances, the Church favors informal, pastoral means for resolving disputes (canons 1446, 1676, 1713-1716, 1733). Judicial and administrative recourse should take place only when pastoral means have been exhausted, or the nature of the matter requires immediate and formal action.

Guidelines that apply to every step

A. Pray. Seek the wisdom of God. Follow the example of the saints and seek their intercession.

B. Know the issue. Study Church documents and other writings on the topic. Our FAITH FACTS are a helpful starting point. They provide relevant citations to sources that are readily available in most Catholic bookstores and parish libraries. The National Conference of Catholic Bishops (NCCB) has various offices that can provide information in their areas of expertise. Its offices include Liturgy, Doctrine, and

Canonical Affairs. Information from one of these offices can be obtained by writing to the following address: (Name of the Office), National Conference of Catholic Bishops, 3211 4th St. N.E., Washington, DC 20017-1194. Use this information to consider objectively and prayerfully the statements made by those with whom you are in conflict. The Apostolic Nuncio also employs a staff to help answer questions. His address is below.

C. The Church presumes good faith unless otherwise proven. You must in charity do the same, careful to give others the benefit of the doubt (cf. Catechism, no. 2478). A contrary approach will likely make matters worse. At all times speak the truth in love (Eph. 4:15), and strive to be an instrument of healing and reconciliation (cf. 2 Cor. 5:18-20).

D. Keep copies of all written materials that pertain to the issue, including letters and decrees. Maintain objective, written records of any meetings, and provide copies of these records to those who participate.

E. The Church favors the principle of subsidiarity. This means that issues are to be resolved at the lowest level possible. Always exhaust the possibility of resolution at the lowest level before moving to the next. Do not involve people who are not part of the solution.

F. During your first contact with higher authority, make him aware of all the relevant facts that pertain to the issue. If possible, provide him with copies of all written materials during this first contact. Without these materials, he cannot objectively consider your request.

Pastoral Procedures

A. As a general rule, at each level noted below, allow at least two weeks and no more than 30 days for the person you contact to respond to your request before contacting him again. After contacting him a second time with no response, move to the next level.

B. Contact the person with whom you have conflict. Discuss your concerns and seek a mutually agreeable resolution. Do not hesitate to meet more than once. Move to the next level of authority only when it becomes evident that no mutual solution will be reached (cf. Mt. 18:15-17).

C. If the first step does not provide a resolution, contact the immediate superior of the person with whom you are in conflict. If the person is an employee of the parish, approach the pastor. If the person is a teacher, contact the principal before approaching the pastor.

D. If the person is the pastor, or if you have already contacted the pastor without success, approach the vicar forane (dean) of your deanery once. He does not have direct authority over the pastor in most circumstances, but he can act as mediator, and in limited instances he can intervene directly (cf. canons 553-55).

E. If the dean is unable to help, find out if your diocese has an office of mediation. The purpose of this office is to assist the faithful in resolving disputes. The dean can direct you to the office of mediation, if one is available.

F. If the office of mediation is unable to assist you in obtaining an agreeable solution, or if your diocese does not have an office of mediation, approach the bishop or one of his vicars according to diocesan protocol. In larger dioceses, particularly those with an archbishop, it is proper to approach a vicar before approaching the bishop. All dioceses have a vicar general. The larger dioceses also have episcopal vicars, who are often bishops. These vicars have direct authority over the priests entrusted to their care. After approaching the vicar, seek the assistance of the bishop himself.

G. If your diocesan bishop is unable to help, and he is not an archbishop, contact the archbishop of your ecclesiastical province once. The archbishop does not have direct authority over the diocesan bishop, but he does have an obligation to help resolve disputes and report abuses to the Holy See (canon 436).

H. After contacting the archbishop without success, contact the Apostolic Nuncio at the following address: Apostolic Nuncio, 3339 Massachusetts Ave. N.W., Washington, DC 20008.

I. If the above approaches prove fruitless, contact the Holy See. If it becomes necessary to take this final step, proper procedures must be used and the matter directed to the proper dicastery (office) of the Holy See, or your request will not be addressed. To obtain assistance in taking this step, contact Information Services at 1-800-693-2484. If we are unable to help you directly, we will refer you to competent persons who can.

Judicial and Administrative Procedures

A. The Church has the exclusive right to judge cases concerning spiritual matters or matters connected with them, particularly those cases that involve violations of ecclesiastical laws, the culpability of sin, and the imposition of ecclesiastical penalties (canon 1401).

B. The purposes of judicial trials within the Church are to prosecute or vindicate rights, ascertain facts (e.g., whether a marriage took place), and impose or declare penalties (canon 1400 §1).

C. The purpose of administrative recourse is to settle controversies that arise from acts of administration within the Church (canon 1400 §2).

D. Both judicial and administrative procedures require specific steps in a particular order. Certain time limits must be followed. If the necessary steps or time limits are not followed, a case can be thrown out.

E. Judicial trials are handled by the diocesan tribunal. Administrative procedures begin by contacting the person whose act caused the controversy. Further appeals must follow the designated procedure.

Canonical advocacy is highly recommended if you find the need to use one of these approaches. Catholics United for the Faith does not provide canonical advocacy. We are able to make referrals to competent persons who can assist you.

Important Point

If you are uncertain as to what course of action to follow, call Information Services (1-800-693-2484), and we can help you determine the best course of action. If judicial or administrative recourse is necessary, we will refer you to competent persons who can assist you.

If a problem remains unresolved despite following this protocol, resist the temptation to speak uncharitably, which will only aggravate the problem. Offer any difficulties as a sacrifice in union with our Eucharistic Lord for your salvation and for the good of the Church. As the late Mother Teresa taught, we are called to be faithful, not successful. Therefore, never grow weary of doing the right thing (cf. 2 Thess. 3:13). Maintain respect for both the person and office of the sacred pastors of the Church, for they act in the person of Christ. It is this genuine fidelity to Christ and His Church that is most effective in fostering authentic renewal. As the fathers of Vatican II explained:

> Each individual layman must be a witness before the world to the resurrection and life of the Lord Jesus, and a sign of the living God. All together, and each one to the best of his ability, must nourish the world with spiritual fruits (cf. Gal. 5:22). They must diffuse in the world the spirit which animates those poor, meek and peace-makers whom the Lord in the Gospel proclaimed blessed (cf. Mt. 5:3-9). In a word: "what the soul is in the body, let Christians be in the world" (LG 38, footnote omitted).